ASIAN CIVILIZATION

L. A. Peter Gosling and William D. Schorger
General Editors

This series of interdisciplinary readings is designed to introduce the western reader to the distinctive components of Asian civilization—social order, political institutions, economic problems, and cultural milieu. Each set of paired volumes contrasts ancient and modern subjects; ageless tradition has been balanced by recent analysis to reveal historical continuity amid the unprecedented change occurring in Asia today.

Albert Feuerwerker, editor of this volume in the Asian Civilization series, is an authority on Chinese economic history. He is the author of *China's Early Industrialization* and co-author of *Chinese Communist Studies of Modern Chinese History.* A graduate of Harvard University, Dr. Feuerwerker is Professor of History and Director of the Center for Chinese Studies at the University of Michigan.

FORTHCOMING TITLES

Traditional India edited by O. L. Chavarria-Aguilar

Modern Southeast Asia edited by John Bastin

The Modern Near East edited by William D. Schorger

The Great Tradition of Asia edited by L. A. Peter Gosling

Modern Japan edited by Roger F. Hackett

Traditional Japan edited by Richard K. Beardsley

MODERN
CHINA

Edited by
Albert Feuerwerker

Prentice-Hall, Inc. *Englewood Cliffs, N.J.*

A SPECTRUM BOOK

Library of Congress Catalog Card Number 64-21957

Printed in the United States of America—C. P 58983, C 58984

CONTENTS

INTRODUCTION

Albert Feuerwerker

The selections in this volume of readings constitute a series of cross sections, at critical points, in the anatomy of China in the last 100 years. They range in time from the mid-nineteenth century— when, in the face of the heightened impact of the West, one might argue that "modern" China began—to the importunate present of the People's Republic of China. In subject matter they focus upon the social, political, economic, and cultural problems that are the threads of modern Chinese history.

With one exception, each of these twelve selections was originally published in 1950 or later, and as a group they are evidence of the interest that Western scholars have taken in China since World War II. They are reprinted here, with the generous permission of the several authors and publishers, in the hope that in this form they may find a wider audience than the relatively restricted group of specialists who first read them in the professional journals or scholarly monographs in which they originally appeared. The pressing need for greater American knowledge of modern China and of the century that went into the making of the regime that now rules from Peking cannot be disputed.

I acknowledge that some readers will not agree that I have chosen the best of all possible selections. I am aware, for example, that for reasons extraneous to the importance of these topics, no materials relating directly to religious developments in modern China, or to the problem of language reform, have been included. (Obliquely, however, some aspects of these topics are encompassed in the articles by Professor Levenson and Mrs. Feuerwerker.)

As a reader, I dislike fragments or vapid condensations; therefore,

1

the number of readings in this book has been limited by a decision to reprint these selections in so far as possible in their entirety. In a few cases, a number of paragraphs of (I fearfully suggest) secondary importance in the present context have been omitted, but in no case has there been any interference of the author's exposition of his arguments in his own words. This has meant, of course, that only items of moderate length could be reprinted. Some pieces quite as good as those included have therefore been arbitrarily excluded. I have, however, chosen to omit all the footnotes that appeared in the original publications. Almost without exception these were references to the sources used by the authors. While important to the specialist, they are perhaps less so to the intelligent layman for whom this volume is compiled. In any case, I believe that the gain of that much more textual material offsets the loss.

The twelve pieces in this volume may be divided into four groups. The first four articles deal with several aspects of Chinese society in the past century. Of the remaining selections, three each are directed to political and economic problems, and the final two are directed to intellectual and cultural developments.

Professor Wright's "Modern China in Transition, 1900-1950" provides a brief but vigorous sketch of the main trends in modern Chinese history and serves as an admirable introduction to the remainder of the volume. Dr. Taeuber's analysis of China's population, past and present, treats what may well be the critical factor in determining the future stability of Communist China. The reader should note that the nationwide birth control campaign that she describes lasted only through 1957, and was precipitately dropped at the beginning of the "Great Leap Forward." Since the summer of 1962, however, there have been numerous signs from Peking that birth control is returning to favor as a government policy. Although the legal age of marriage has not been changed, Peking now publicly frowns on early marriages. Also, the press has been publishing frank articles by medical experts on various contraceptive methods, but there has not yet returned anything like the fervor of 1957. Dr. Freedman's article discusses the changing structure and function of the Chinese family during the past century, and also provides a more concrete picture of the kinship units that Dr. Taeuber has treated statistically. The way of life of the 80 per cent or more of the Chinese population who are peasants is treated in Dr. Buck's "Chinese Agriculture." This is not so much an analysis of economic relations in rural China as a description of what peasant life was like in the 1920's and 1930's, and to a great extent for a whole century before. Some of Dr. Buck's data—for example, with regard to land ownership—are disputed by other observers, but the general picture is a reliable one.

The next three articles treat in turn aspects of the Chinese state and government under the Manchu dynasty in the nineteenth century; under the Nationalist Government, 1927-1949; and during the first decade of the Communist People's Republic of China. Professor Michael's article centers on an analysis of the critical role of the "scholar-gentry" in the imperial state. It should be pointed out that this is a subject of considerable controversy among specialists, and that some of Professor Michael's conclusions, based in part on the admirable studies of the nineteenth-century gentry by Chang Chung-li, run counter to the frequently held opinion that stresses the close relationship between the position and power of the Chinese gentry and landownership. Dr. Ch'ien's *The Government and Politics of China,* from which his chapter on the Kuomintang is reprinted, is a landmark in the modern study of Chinese government. The undisputed importance of the Kuomintang (Nationalist Party) in the history of the Republic of China makes this chapter a particularly critical one in understanding the failure of the Nationalist Government to achieve a unified and reconstructed China. Although Dr. Ch'ien's account deals only with the period prior to 1949, it is also of significance that the Kuomintang, under largely the same leadership and with its San Min Chu I ideology unaltered, continues as the ruling party on Taiwan. The article by Professor Schurmann is not a study of the formal governmental structure of Communist China; it is rather an analysis of the changing organizational modes that the Chinese Communists have employed since 1949 in their efforts to transform China into a modern industrialized power. To some extent, any discussion of current developments in the People's Republic of China is dated almost as soon as it appears. In spite of the suddenness with which the scene is likely to change in Peking, Professor Schurmann's conclusions continue to be valid as of the end of 1962.

The three articles which are devoted to the Chinese economy should be read in conjunction with Dr. Buck's description of Chinese agriculture. My chapter on some aspects of the Chinese economy in the latter half of the nineteenth century is part of a larger study of the *kuan-tu shang-pan* (official supervision and merchant management) type of enterprise that characterized China's early industrialization efforts. I suggest that these are the forerunners of the "bureaucratic capitalism" of the republican period. Dr. Paauw's study of the economic policies of the Nationalist Government is in part concerned with that bureaucratic capitalism as an obstacle to economic development. Professor Schran, in turn, offers an analysis of the economic policies which the Chinese Communist authorities have utilized since 1949, and of Peking's successes and failures.

Professor Levenson's article is a stimulatingly fresh assault on the problem of the intellectual changes that have both accompanied and inspired other aspects of China's modern revolution. Mrs. Feuerwerker looks more closely at one of the more interesting sides of the intellectual revolution: the development of modern Chinese literature.

Individually, and as a group, these articles link China's past century with her importunate present and suggest what the continuities and radical changes have been. In this volume are some sharp perspectives on modern China.

1

MODERN CHINA IN TRANSITION,
1900=1950

Mary C. Wright

Most Americans had little occasion to think seriously about China
until Communist China began to emerge as a major power. Even
those who were especially interested in China seldom gave systematic
attention to the current scene. Scholars nearly all studied periods
before—usually very long before—1900. Missionaries, government
officials, businessmen, and military personnel were absorbed in pressing daily tasks. Most lacked the training, even if they had the time
and inclination, to observe perceptively and to gauge accurately the
momentous changes occurring around them. A handful of journalists
made outstanding efforts to find out what was really happening, to
set it in its epochal context, and to report it in readable English.
Yet even among these, a working knowledge of the Chinese language
and a familiarity with recent Chinese history were rarities. No one
doubted that a grasp of the background was essential, but the
background grasped was a strange blend of conflicting myths that
have remained to block our comprehension of contemporary China.

COLLAPSE OF THE MIDDLE KINGDOM

Everywhere in the world the headlong changes that marked the
first half of the twentieth century dwarfed the slower changes of
earlier centuries, but nowhere did these changes so stagger the

Dr. Wright, Professor of History, Yale University, is the author of *The
Last Stand of Chinese Conservatism: The T'ung-chih Restoration, 1862-
1874* (1957), and of many articles on modern and recent Chinese history.
This article is reprinted with permission from *The Annals of the American Academy of Political and Social Science* (January 1959), 1-8. Copyright © 1959 by The American Academy of Political and Social Science.

imagination as in China. The longest lived and most populous polity in world history had changed so slowly over millennia that sometimes it seemed not to have changed at all. Certainly there had been nothing remotely comparable to the steady and accelerating transformation of European life beginning in the late Middle Ages. Then suddenly and nearly simultaneously China was struck with equivalents of the Reformation, the French Revolution, and the Russian Revolution. Marx and Darwin were new, but no newer than Aristotle and Rousseau. Young Chinese discovered them all at the same time.

This unprecedented telescoping of history was at first obscured by the continued and obviously vigorous persistence of the many ancient ways that so delighted all visitors. In the midst of a living antiquity unparalleled in the modern world, the signs of the progressive stages of a great revolution were generally discounted. Our experience had not prepared us for a society marked both by strong tradition and by powerful revolutionary drives. The signs of tradition were plain to see and comforting. The signs of revolution could be dismissed as superficial. There were such very wide troughs between the waves that at the time we could not see that there was any cumulative buildup. Today in retrospect, the classic French and Russian sequence is clearly outlined. The Chinese timetable, however, was so different that by the time we began to suspect that we might be seeing the beginning of a great social revolution, the revolution was already far advanced.

The basic thread of Chinese history during the first half of the twentieth century was the search—sometimes ebullient, often heartbroken—for new institutions in every sphere of public and private life, institutions which would connect the pride in a great past to high hopes for a great future. In the tumultuous controversies of fifty years, the Chinese centered their attention on one or another facet of a few great questions: What of the old is worth keeping? Can we keep it and survive in the modern world? What of the new is desirable? Must we take the undesirable too in order to survive? Or can China make a future for herself on lines not yet tried elsewhere? These questions were of mounting urgency, for the Chinese state was prostrate and Chinese life seemed to be disintegrating.

THE FORCE OF NATIONALISM

Because vigorous nationalism provides built-in incentives which a successful government can use to spur and control its people, the growth of nationalism was one of the most significant features of China's recent history. When the twentieth century opened, the power of the Chinese Empire was a very recent and live memory. Hence the shattering series of stunning defeats at the hands of the Western powers and Japan was especially galling. We did not give enough attention to the sharp and swift rise of fighting nationalism. Daily observation of the polite and humorous Chinese, plus a little dabbling in Chinese philosophy, led to the myth that the Chinese were only interested in their own families, that they had no conception of country. Everyone could tell a story to illustrate the point, from the embassy to the kitchen level. Opposite conclusions were drawn from this alleged basic characteristic of twentieth-century China: The Chinese were venal and lacking in decent feeling for the public good, or the Chinese were charming sages happily free of the lusts for power that had wrecked what had been European civilization until 1914. But in either case, the basic analysis was dreadfully faulty.

There was in fact a genuine ground swell of Chinese nationalism during the first half of the twentieth century, and for its element of xenophobia there were clear historic roots. So much has been written lately of Chinese popular good will toward foreigners until they were brain-washed en masse that, at the risk of gross oversimplification, something should also be said of Chinese bitterness and hatred toward Americans and Europeans in recent decades. The crude fear of the white peril that the last imperial dynasty had been able to exploit in the Boxer Rebellion of 1900 had been submerged but not overcome, and the expanding special privileges of foreigners were irritants in increasingly wide spheres of Chinese life. These fears and irritations provided a mass sounding board for what might otherwise have been rather arid denunciations of imperialists. It is well to remember that both Nationalists and Communists have struck this note; that Chiang Kai-shek and Lenin described the tangible effects of imperialism in remarkably similar terms.

THE SEARCH FOR POLITICAL STABILITY

The increasingly patent ineffectiveness of political leadership and institutions was a no less important characteristic of twentieth-century China. This phenomenon was obvious to all, but it was misinterpreted because we did not attach enough importance to the fact that political decline was accompanied by repeated efforts to reconstitute a powerful central government. When government was weakest, the pressures for strong government were greatest, for it was then that both traditional culturalism and modern nationalism were most offended. The various movements and programs that expressed these pressures struck us as rather silly, and the myth grew that Chinese politics was horseplay among warlords with silver bullets. Warlordism was, of course, a fact, but we were wrong to conclude from this that the Chinese people opposed strong government or that no central power could be effective throughout so vast and undeveloped a country. The imperial tradition of strong central government never died, and now in retrospect one is struck by how much authority the central government did in fact retain until 1917. Even the "warlord period," 1917-27, was no era of general collapse of centralized authority, for the warlords themselves operated effective political machines over substantial territories. More important, the major contenders for power aimed consistently at the reconstitution of a powerful central state. As external dangers and internal crises mounted, the population of the country did not remain as apathetic and cynical as was thought in Treaty Port circles. On the record of performance it is clear that increasingly wide sectors of the population were prepared to throw their support to whoever gave most promise of effective central government.

The terrible strains of the period notwithstanding, the country remained vigorous, and tremendous new potentials were created in spite of war and inadequate leadership. We were too given to pity for a suffering and downtrodden people, and the pity irked. Widespread suffering there was indeed, but at its lowest point twentieth-century China was no beaten and stagnant country. Rather it offered the world the remarkable spectacle of a people whose ancient institutions had retained great vigor and effectiveness until very recent times; a people with a well-justified pride in the record of a great and prosperous state as well as in their intellectual and artistic heritage; a people who were learning modern skills rapidly and well and yet who with all this promise felt themselves in danger of national extinction because they had found no way to mobilize this latent strength for defense against aggression and foreign special privilege, for raising the standard of living, for a cultural renascence.

AGRARIAN CHINA: PEASANTS AND POLITICS

During the first half of the twentieth century, China remained an overwhelmingly agricultural country. Although the proportionate position of the agrarian sector of the economy declined somewhat, the peasant's produce remained the chief source of revenue, and his tax burden increased steadily with the rising cost of more elaborate arms, proliferating government offices, and the service of foreign loans. The terms of rural credit were devastating and tenancy increased, especially in the vicinity of modernized cities. The increased acreage planted in cash crops undermined the traditional self-sufficiency of the village, and cottage industries, once an important source of supplementary income, either disappeared or were bought by merchants. The self-employed artisan all but disappeared, and there was little to mitigate the harsh consequences of the imbalance between the high market value of manufactured goods and the low market value of agricultural products.

No patriotic Chinese could remain insensitive to the plight of the peasant base of society, even if the interest was only theoretical. The programs of the warlords regularly mentioned the need for reforms. The Kuomintang, which came to power in 1927, also had an elaborate rural program; its implementation was unfortunately delayed until threats from the Chinese Communists and from Japan could be removed. Perhaps more important as a symptom of the same kind of guilty uneasiness that drove prerevolutionary Russian intellectuals into populist movements, there was a rash of local experiments in rural reconstruction, sparked mainly by liberals of the minor parties whose programs lay somewhere between the Kuomintang and Communist poles. These efforts were important signs of the times; yet the country was so vast that major accomplishment could not really have been expected without strong government support. They were obliterated in the holocaust of the Japanese invasion.

One barrier to the implementation of the Kuomintang land reform program was the landed wealth of its members. There were exceptions of course, especially among Kuomintang members from the modern business and professional classes. Even among these, however, there was fear that a land reform program, once launched, might gain too much momentum and turn against the Kuomintang. After 1937, with the loss to Japan of the modern cities these men represented, the Kuomintang became increasingly dependent upon the rural economy and thus upon the support of ultraconservative landlords in the hinterland.

Meanwhile, the Chinese Communist Party, founded in 1921, moved rather quickly away from the classic Marxian distrust of the peasantry. The party line shifted tortuously on this as on other points, yet within a few years Mao Tse-tung and others were demonstrating their skill in peasant agitation. Kuomintang realization that peasants when aroused would almost certainly swing to the Communists was a major cause of the breakup of the first Kuomintang-Communist united front and of the Kuomintang's swing to the right after 1927. Driven back into the countryside by the victorious Nationalist armies, the Communists began a long series of land reform experiments, varying according to circumstances from moderate rent reduction to wholesale confiscation. By degrees the Communist party learned how to mobilize peasant support. The Chinese peasant loved his land, but by the third and fourth decades of the twentieth century it could no longer keep him alive without radical changes, and only the Communists offered these.

During the civil war, 1946-49, the Communists succeeded in using land reform as a major political and military weapon. The national government, threatened on all sides, was not prepared to take any very drastic steps. The Chinese-American Joint Committee on Rural Reconstruction struggled manfully to improve agrarian technology in the hope that, with an increased harvest, the peasant's plight could be eased without damage to landlord interests. The conclusion of the outstanding Chinese official chiefly responsible for the effort was that nearly everywhere technological change proved impossible without fundamental institutional change; that indeed without social reform, the peasant could not take advantage of improved methods, and his position often actually deteriorated.

URBAN DEVELOPMENTS

Before 1950, the modern sectors of the Chinese economy lagged so far behind the West, Japan, and even India that one did not usually notice how great the development had been between 1900 and 1950. Beginning in the 1890's, Chinese of a new type, scholar-officials who were also entrepreneurs, began to build substantial modern factories. Mining, railroads, and shipping developed rapidly. The physical plant, the labor force, the managers and technicians required for a modern economy began to appear in increasing numbers. The potential was there for anyone to see, and yet it could not be realized. To the Chinese, this was infuriating. The chief barriers seemed to be inept and predatory government, fragments of traditional social institutions, drainage from the country of the profits from the enormous foreign investment in China, and the special protection that the unequal treaties provided for foreign interests, often directly against Chinese interests. Many Chinese businessmen, who enjoyed a boom while privileged Western competition was deflected by World War I, became in a sense revolutionaries, precisely because they were patriots and businessmen. They supported the Kuomintang in its bid for power, 1924-27, because of its program to abolish imperialism; to create an effective, modern, centralized government; and to campaign relentlessly against the shreds of the Confucian order.

During this period, strikes and other signs of labor unrest were widespread, especially in foreign-owned enterprises. The foreigners' customary retort that their labor was at all events much better paid than other Chinese labor was irrelevant. Chinese peasants coming to work in factories for the first time suddenly saw much greater gaps between poverty and wealth than they had ever seen before. The poverty, and it was still extreme poverty by any standards, was theirs; the wealth belonged to foreigners and to a few Chinese who could readily be labeled "running dogs of the foreigners," and it was often displayed in a manner that could scarcely have been better calculated to offend.

This frustration was felt in many spheres of Chinese society. The professional diplomats of China, skilled though many of them were, made only limited and gradual progress toward abolishing the unequal international status that outraged Chinese of every political persuasion. The Japanese invasion of the mainland struck at the very core of China's national integrity, and the international complications of the war period left a tangled legacy of misapprehensions and misunderstanding. Western relinquishment of extraterritorial privileges during the war came far too late, and the continuing major role of the United States in the postwar period convinced many Chinese that the national government was incapable of independent action. To these Chinese, the situation seemed further proof that diplomatic resources, like economic resources, were useless to a weak government and that military power was essential to political effectiveness.

THE KEY ROLE OF MILITARY POWER

The new importance attached to military power was another major characteristic of modern Chinese history. Chinese had never been the pacifists that we often fondly imagined them to be, and it had been clear to them since their first contact with the military power of the West that only a country with strong armed forces could elect its own policies. For a century there was a steady sequence of military reorganization programs. Every program failed; never was the required fighting strength achieved; never was a war won. Yet what was accomplished in inadequate bits and pieces convinced nearly all Chinese that China need not forever be a pawn in world politics; that there were no insuperable obstacles to genuine great power status. Experience had shown that Chinese peasants could be trained to use modern weapons efficiently and that they could on occasion fight with unsurpassed valor. Why was the opposite so often the case? Experience had shown that the country had the natural resources and the technological aptitudes needed for a modern arms industry. Why had one not developed? China had a small number of skilled strategists and effective line officers. Why were they not better deployed, and why had not many times their number been trained? The popular feeling as defeat followed defeat was less one of despair than of anger at the waste of opportunity. To a desperate government, massive outside aid seemed the only answer. To many Chinese, so much foreign aid to so weak a government seemed bound to lead to spiraling dependence. The suggestion that this was the intention of the aid fell on ready ears.

EDUCATION

Some observers insisted that the Chinese attitudes described above were limited to a tiny and powerless fraction of the population. They failed to note how rapidly political awareness was spreading through education and propaganda. It would be difficult to find any period in the history of any country where education was expected to work the miracles it was expected to work in twentieth-century China, and very nearly did. The dominant Chinese tradition, in marked contrast to Western tradition, had always held that men are by nature good and that although their talents vary, the variation has nothing to do with class. Hence education, on which an enormous value was placed, was theoretically as desirable for the lower classes as for the upper. It had always been gratifying rather than terrifying to see the son of a peasant attain a high education with all its consequent rewards. His chance to do this was slim indeed, but the barrier was economic only.

With the twentieth century, the peasant's chance at education began to improve rapidly. The missionary schools and the new government schools provided only a fraction of the facilities that would have been required for universal public education. Even so, they were closer to such a system than they were to the traditional system of tutors and academies. The way seemed open in the not too distant future for every Chinese to be given a basic education and for the ablest Chinese to be given the highest education. But to attain this end, vigorous government action was needed. Successive governments made some contribution, but only under heavy pressure from the leaders of public opinion. Education had a low priority on all budgets, and as new ideas mushroomed, some of those in power came to cherish an illiterate population. Mass education movements found contrived obstacles rather than the support they needed. Too many schools remained under foreign control, and it was humiliating to realize how dreadfully the foreign schools were needed. There was almost no field in which China offered full advanced training, this despite the world renown of many of her scholars, once they were trained abroad.

THE CHANCES FOR DEMOCRACY

Thus in education as in other fields, progress led not to stable satisfaction but to a sharpening awareness of how much more had to be done, and, it was believed, could be done, if China had an effective and efficient government. There were fifty years of controversy over the kind of government China had and the kind of government she needed. The trends were frequently confusing, for in China political characteristics that the West regarded as inevitably associated were often in conflict, and others that the West regarded as mutually incompatible were sometimes fused.

During the first half of the twentieth century, the trend toward democracy was strong in China—in some senses of the word. Legally privileged classes had already disappeared, and as the upper classes continued to expand rapidly in size, there were in China millions of families of some little importance rather than a few hundred very powerful ones. The open classes of the traditional society became highly fluid during a period of such rapid change. The country had since early times been culturally homogeneous, vertically as well as horizontally. Of course there were popular cultures, elite cultures, and subcultures, but nothing resembling the cultural cleavage between classes that until recently characterized much of Europe. With the spread of modern public education, few cultural stigmata of class origin remained. Traditionally, popular opinion had been taken seriously by the government, and after 1919 the media for its expression expanded like the burst of a Roman candle.

In all these meanings—and they are valid meanings—twentieth-century China was democratic, and increasingly democratic. Yet this trend toward democracy lacked two elements considered essential in the West. There was no trend toward the establishment of civil liberties and there was no trend toward government by majority decision.

Neither of the two major political movements—the Nationalist and the Communist—showed any real interest in civil liberties, or even comprehension of what they were. As in traditional China, whatever purported to be the interests of the group remained paramount. In the 1920's there were flurries of talk about civil liberties, mainly among intellectuals, but these were crushed from both left and right. In the 1930's and 1940's, internal crises and foreign aggression seemed to require unfettered action by a powerful government if there was to be a viable future for anyone Chinese. In such circumstances, it is not surprising that a demand for civil liberties came to seem a demand for a right to wilful self-indulgence. There was no thought that individual Chinese ought to be guaranteed some small but irreducible minimum of privacy and originality, an area that the state could never touch, however great the alleged public interest.

Nor was there any trend toward representative government in the first half of the twentieth century. In Chinese tradition there had never been any notion that the wisest decision could be reached by counting heads, even in a select group. Statesmanship had been the art of selecting, training, and indoctrinating a small corps of able men who could then be trusted to run every aspect of the public life of a vast empire. To secure popular assent to official decision was essential; to ask the people what the decision should be never remotely occurred to anyone. Within the official hierarchy there were intricate checks and balances, impeachments, conferences, and compromises, but no idea of majority decision. After 1912, the few efforts at a façade of parliamentary government were fiascos, and most Chinese of all political persuasions saw the main problem as the creation of a competent new political elite to fill the gap left by the collapse of the imperial system. The idea of military tutelage followed by political tutelage meant exercise of power on behalf of the people by a nonhereditary, authoritarian political corps. It was as basic to Nationalist as to Communist political thought. During the first half of the century, neither party relinquished its control to popular elections. In 1950, the promise of ultimate full democracy offered by either seemed remote.

2

CHINA'S POPULATION:
RIDDLE OF THE PAST,
ENIGMA OF THE FUTURE

Irene B. Taeuber

When, on November 1, 1954, the People's Republic of China announced that it had more than 600 million people, the ancient riddle of the demographers escaped the confines of academic controversy. A census figure became a newspaper headline. In distant places there were prophecies of the doom that awaited a people as numerous as the Chinese; but among China's neighbors there were intensified fears of infiltration and inundation. The statistical damage was devastating, for if China had 600 million people in 1954, she had had approximately that many people for a considerable period of time. If the scholarly studies of recent decades had been based on false premises, the estimates of the past trends and the prewar status of the population of China were alike erroneous.

The population of China is far more than that of a nation. The Chinese are the largest group of ethnically and culturally unified people on the earth's surface; they constitute one fourth of the world's population. All other demographic facts and processes in the Pacific area are ripples on the currents of Asian and world developments if assessed against the magnitude of the size and potential growth of the Chinese people. The basic questions transcend the demographic. Is a population such as that claimed by the Chinese Communists an explosive force or a protean mass whose planned expansions and undirected movements alike threaten its

Since 1936 Dr. Taeuber has been Research Associate, Office of Population Research, Princeton University. She was co-editor of *Population Index*, 1935-1954. Among her latest works are *The Population of Japan* (1958); and, with Conrad Taeuber, *The Changing Population of the United States, 1790-1955* (1958). This article is reprinted with permission from *The Antioch Review*, Vol. 17, No. 1 (March 1957), 7-17. Copyright © 1957 by The Antioch Press.

neighbors? Or does this immense population with its present density and its great potential for growth doom the Chinese themselves to a life where hunger, ignorance, and their associated instabilities preclude either substantial economic advance or enduring political power?

THE CENSUS-REGISTRATION OF 1953-1954

The quest for the significance of a population of 602 million Chinese for Mainland China, Asia, and the world has a necessary prelude in technical description and evaluation. The question is one of fact. Did or did not the People's Republic of China have a population of 602 million as of midnight on June 30, 1953? More precise formulation is possible. The Communists' total figure includes estimates of 7.6 million Chinese in Taiwan and 11.7 million other Chinese outside Mainland China. The question thus becomes that of the survey procedures that yielded a population of 583 million for Mainland China itself. The area of China is great, the terrain is difficult, and communication facilities are limited. Most of the people are illiterate, and they are suspicious of government inquisitions for whatever purpose. The interrelated problems of organization, reporting, and processing had precluded accurate nationwide registration or enumeration of the population by any previous government of China.

The plans and procedures for the census of 1953 were quite sophisticated, for Peking itself had many statisticians and there was technical assistance from the Soviet Union. Major attention was given to the organization for enumeration, the schedules were simple, and the results were hand-tabulated at local levels and transmitted upward in the administrative hierarchy for progressive summation. The inquiry was limited to the essential items of residence, age, sex, and nationality; the party apparatus was utilized at national, provincial, and local levels. In densely settled localities people came to the census offices to register, whereas in dispersed areas there was field enumeration. (Some eight million pople in minority areas were not individually enumerated. In addition, the figure of 7.6 million was accepted for Taiwan. Data on overseas Chinese were collected by the Committee on the Affairs of the Chinese Population Living Abroad.) All information was to be as of the critical date of June 30, 1953; residence was to be the place of permanent residence rather than the place of enumeration. Major difficulties arose in the determination of residence and of age, however, and migration presented many complications. An ingenious device of a discarded section of the schedule permitted families to report their long-absent members without disturbing the tabulations of a habitually resident population. Temporarily absent persons were reported by and included with their families; persons temporarily present were not registered or enumerated. The destination cards which all migrants are required to carry were marked to indicate previous inclusion in the counting.

Age presented even greater difficulties than residence, for there is no commonly accepted uniform year in China, and traditional Chinese do not reckon age in completed years by counting the newborn infant as zero years of age. Reported age might be in the Western system of reckoning or in the Chinese system whereby the infant is one year of age at birth and ages a year at the New Year. In the latter case, year of birth might be given in terms of the cycles of the years or in terms of the years of the dynastic reign. Census personnel carried elaborate forms in order to transform reported year of birth to age in completed years. Both the reports on census operations and the fragmentary data available by age indicate that the Communist statisticians did not solve the problem of age reporting in a mixed Western-lunar system.

All the intricate procedures for the allocation of residence, the counting of migrants once and only once, and the determination of age meant delays in enumeration and tabulation. Finally the requirement of reference to the critical date as of June 30, 1953, and the elaborate instructions as to residence and age were relaxed. The time schedule required that provincial totals be available by November, 1953. By the end of 1953 the census was reported as 29 per cent completed. In the following March it was reported that the census had been completed in 30 per cent of the country. At this time orders were issued that procedures be simplified and the census completed quickly. In June, the Deputy Prime Minister announced the general results; in November, the Statistics Bureau made an official report.

How accurate were the data secured in this census-registration of 1953-1954? No information on procedures and no data now available permit a definitive answer. The Statistics Office claimed phenomenal accuracy on the basis of "on-the-spot control checks" of 53 million people; but casual acceptance of the claim is not possible for those who know the lack of quantitative awareness among the

Chinese and the characteristics of China. Comparisons of Communist and Nationalist figures indicate gross discrepancies, but the known deficiencies of the Nationalist data are such that disagreements with them constitute no basis either for acceptance or for repudiation. The Communist government has developed various registration and reporting systems, particularly household registers that provide for the recording of births, deaths, out-movements, and in-movements. The total and the provincial populations as estimated for 1953 agree rather closely with those presumably secured from the census-registration. This agreement does not constitute validation of either series, but instead raises serious questions as to the degree of independence between the records, the estimated populations, and the census enumerations at the local levels. Thus proper caution would dictate suspended judgment as to the completeness and accuracy of the census-registration of 1953-1954. However, the suspension of judgment would be of long duration, for it would have to last until such a time as the government in Peking published the detailed data for all China, the provinces, the *hsien,* and the major cities. It is necessary, therefore, that some general decision as to validity be made on the basis of the fragments of information now available. Acceptance of all the data as essentially correct for all characteristics in all areas would be naïve indeed, but total rejection would be contrary to many known facts. The balance of the present evidence suggests that the activities of 1953-1954 were the nearest to a count that has been made of the population of China. As such, the results must be accepted provisionally for operational and planning purposes. It should be noted that the Communist government itself has accepted them.

THE QUESTIONS OF THE PAST AND PRESENT

If the population of Mainland China was about 600 million in 1953-1954, it must have been approximately this size in the days before the war with Japan, World War II, and the revolution. This large a population in the early 1930's is quite inconsistent with the official figures of the time, and thus also quite inconsistent with the accepted reconstructions of the growth of China's population in recent centuries. To pursue this topic through the morass of conflicting evidence and alternative estimates is impossible here. A comparison of the official reports of population in the Ch'ing dynasty with those of the Communists suggests that the size of the present population is not unduly large if these past figures are accepted as reasonably close to the realities of the time. The population of the Ch'ing dynasty was reported as 265 million in 1775; 295 million in 1800; 380 million in 1825; and 430 million in 1850. The population in the years from 1930 to 1950 was approximately 580 million. Thus population increased about 150 million in the years from 1775 to 1850, and then increased another 150 million in the years from 1850 to 1930-1950. The magnitude of these increases is tremendous, but the rates of the increase were low, and over long periods of time they were declining.

The slow but irregular growth of the Chinese population in the past reflected the changing differences between high and fluctuating death rates and high but fairly stable birth rates. The major variable was the death rate, and the major factors in that variable were the adequacy of food, the prevalence of disease, and the level of internal order. Famine, epidemic, and revolution were the great deterrents to consistent growth. The long period of growth from the middle-eighteenth to the middle-nineteenth centuries was associated with the administrative efficiency of the Ch'ing dynasty and the economic advances promoted by it. New crops from the Americas, movements into less developed areas, and more intensive cultivation provided food for the increasing population. Epidemics continued, but there seem to have been few of the great pandemics or natural calamities that decimate the populations of great regions.

Some time about the middle of the nineteenth century the complex of relationships favoring population growth seems to have encountered the cumulative calamities of the period of decline. The Taiping Rebellion of the 1850's ended the effective administrative control of the central government. A greatly increased population, inefficient administration, and precarious order were associated with a widened prevalence of malnutrition, famine, and epidemic. The great new forces limiting mortality in the colonial areas of Asia were largely absent from China. The industrial and commercial penetration of the West extended little beyond the cities. Public health services, agricultural experiment stations, elementary education—these were known to few of China's uncounted millions. Life remained in the patterns of old. Premature death was so prevalent that only the abundant child-bearing of a Confucian and ancestor-venerating people prevented population decline, if indeed decline was not episodic over great regions of the country. In periods of crisis the brake of mortality on population growth extended even to birth itself, for the poor disposed of the infants for whom they could not provide.

This control of population growth by death characterized all the peoples of Asia in the premodern period, and it characterizes all except the Japanese today. Death rates were reduced earlier in the colonial areas than they were in China, and the rates were reduced further. Birth rates remained at their premodern levels, and so population growth began earlier and was more rapid in the colonial areas than in China. Thus China's very backwardness in the past reduced the rate of growth and prevented the development of a population much larger than the one that now exists.

This reconstruction of the past dynamics of the Chinese population is based more on historical description than on accurate measurement. Its essential validity is corroborated by all the statistics that have been collected and all the studies that have been made of Chinese within China or on her peripheries.

The present levels of birth and death rates and hence the present rate of natural increase are as little known as those of the past. In 1954 the Communists announced that a survey of vital rates among 30 million people showed a birth rate of 37 per 1,000 total population and a death rate of 17. The rate of natural increase was thus two per cent per year. The birth rate of 37 is quite inconsistent with the results of previous studies of the fertility of the Chinese; the death rate of 17 is quite suspect on the basis of the known limitations to public health activities in modern China. The underestimation of births and deaths alike leaves little basis for assessing the probability of a rate of natural increase of two per cent at the time of the survey. For instance, a birth rate of 47 and a death rate of 27 are rather plausible, and this combination would yield an annual rate of increase of two per cent.

GROWTH AND ITS RELATIONSHIPS

Whatever happened in the past, and whatever the precise rate of natural increase at the moment, the outlines of current problems are fairly clear. Mainland China has a gigantic population, and its growth potential is great. The assessment of present relations and future prospects would not be altered greatly if the population were 50 to 100 million above or below the number reported in the census-registration of 1953-1954. The reason for this seeming irrelevance of the absolute number of Chinese at a specific date is the admitted magnitude of the number and the magnitude of the annual increases that may occur if conditions are such as to permit the reductions of death rates that are technically possible. The government of the Republic of China reported the population of China as 463,493,000 in 1948; the Communist figure for 1953 is 582,603,-000. The experience of many other areas indicates that the elimination of famines and epidemics combined with the sparing but efficient use of DDT and the antibiotics could reduce the death rate to 15 per 1,000 total population. If the birth rate is about 45, the reduction of the death rate to 15 without changes in the birth rate would leave a natural increase of 30. If the Nationalist estimate of 463 million is accepted, a rate of natural increase of three per cent would add 13.9 million people to the population in a year. Less than a decade would be required for this population of 463 million to reach the Communist figure of 583 million. If the Communist population of 583 million is accepted, a rate of natural increase of three percent would add 17.6 million people to the population in a year.

Manipulations of estimates—population size, assumed present and future growth rates—could be continued almost indefinitely. But the critical question is not the numbers *per se* but the meaning of an attained size and growth potential such as that of China for the social transformation, economic development, and political stability of the country. In the long run, the critical questions are those involving the trend in the growth rate, and particularly the possibility that the rate of increase may be reduced quickly and the period of growth that accompanies economic modernization shortened. Overshadowing all these somewhat hypothetical queries is this very real question: Can China, vast in space and numbers, with agrarian pressures on her resources, develop industrially and maintain her power without exacting the incalculable human costs of selective exterminations?

The estimate of China's growth potential was only the roughest of approximations, for actual growth depends on the difference between birth and death rates. These rates are not predictable, either separately or in combination. The future course of each is dependent on the economic and social changes that occur in China; these changes, in turn, are reciprocally affected by the course of death and birth rates, and by the extent of the population increase as it relates to the use of old and new resources dedicated to raising the level of living for the Chinese people.

The reduction of the death rate is a question of the feasible rather than of the policies of government and the aspirations of people. The reduction of disease and the prevention of premature death are almost obsessive goals of the governments and peoples of Asia, and the Mainland Chinese are no exception. What can be done in health services and public sanitation must be done; people who realize that disease can be eradicated, death prevented, do not remain quiescent while the scourges continue. Moreover, economic advances in agriculture and in industry require vigorous people rather than those debilitated by disease and weakened by hunger. In the abstract, therefore, it might seem that Communist China would follow the example of Ceylon, that DDT and all the modern miracle chemicals would be applied throughout the land, that death rates would drop quickly from Eastern to Western levels. The situation is not so simple. The provision of public health services for 500 to 600 or 700 million people requires immense investments in facilities and personnel. The chemicals and the medicines must be produced or imported, and neither is yet possible in sufficient quantities.

If the increase in food production and in general economic development proceeds rapidly enough to insure rising levels of nutrition and of income for the increasing numbers of people, death rates can be expected to decline. The rate of that decline would be related to the extent of the resources devoted to health and sanitary activities. There are circular relations here. The economic development that proceeds more rapidly than population growth permits rising levels of living and government investments in health activities, thus reducing death rates. Failure in economic development, particularly in the agricultural sector, could mean not alone the failure of death rates to decline but the recurrence in even greater magnitude of the great famines and other forms of decimation.

The problems of reducing and of reduced mortality are necessary and continuing ones for Communist China, as for other areas in roughly similar economic-demographic situations. If the birth rate is 45 per 1,000 total population, growth occurs unless the death rate is also 45. Yet development is inconceivable in the physical, social, and economic situation that generates death rates of 45. On the other hand, the greater the economic development, the more rapid the extension of the new health miracles and the more rapid the decline of the death rate—and the greater the economic development required simply to provide for the increased population. The simple arithmetic of the relations between economic growth and population increase dictates that eventually either the economic growth slows and then ceases because of the pressures of population, or the population increase slows and then ceases, thus permitting the continuation of economic growth. The increase of the death rate would retard economic growth. It would indeed represent economic failure. It is not a feasible solution to the economic problems of population growth. The only solution to those problems is the decline of population increase through the reduction of the birth rate.

The question of the birth rate, in China as elsewhere, has been surrounded with charges and countercharges of Malthusianism and Neo-Malthusianism, of Marxian ideology versus capitalistic theories, of optimists versus pessimists in population-resources relationships of the present and the future. Chinese Communists were blatant Marxians in their first years in power; they remain so today, but with a critical difference. They now condemn Neo-Malthusianism on economic grounds but advocate population control on social and political grounds. The origin of this characteristically Chinese handling of a problem of rational behavior seems to lie in the coincidence of the census results and the operational plans for development in the various sectors of the society and economy. For instance, education is essential to the development of the industrial, urban, and politically conscious population. The building of schools, the production of supplies, and the training of teachers for a nation of 450 million or so inhabitants seemed a stupendous task. Suddenly the population for which schools had to be provided became 583 million. And then the official survey indicated a two per cent rate of population increase—12 million additional people each year. The rational policy seemed to require a reduction in the rate of increase, but the only way in which this rate could be lessened was through a reduction of the birth rate. This the Chinese decided to accomplish.

Actions came swiftly once the relation between high birth rates and the success of party programs became apparent. The initial speech came in Peking in the fall of 1954. In 1955 a party theorist demonstrated the need for a limitation of births in terms of the health of women and children, the provision of time for study and party work, and the opportunities that responsible parents owed their children. The official journals of the All China Federation of Democratic Women and the Communist Youth League ran major articles on birth control and recommended its practice. Contraceptive supplies were placed on sale. The laws on abortion and sterilization were liberalized. Studies of the traditional remedies of the herbalists were authorized. The Minister of Health seemingly wavered in her decisions, but on June 19, 1956, she apologized to the National People's Congress for her failures and on August 6 she directed all health officers to push the campaign to spread information about birth control techniques.

THE ENIGMA OF THE FUTURE

The assessment of the population statistics and the policy statements of Communist China are alike difficult. Even complete information on census and vital statistics data and complete reports on the policy activities would be an inadequate basis for predicting the future growth of the population. The initial reactions of students involve skepticism about the statistics and cynicism about the policies. Admitting that the census is an approximate count, and that birth rates are very high, there remains the question of the present level and the future course of the death rate. Given industrial development, increasing food production, expanding health services, and declining death rates, there remains the question of the trend in the birth rate. Unless that birth rate declines sooner and more swiftly than it did with industrialization and urbanization in the West and in Japan, economic development itself may be slowed, the decline of mortality retarded or erased, and so the forces stimulating declining birth rates blunted. A more rapid decline of fertility requires the adoption of planned parenthood by the peasants in the villages, for only thus can national population growth be reduced appreciably except in the very long run. And few students would argue that China has a very long run in which to solve the problems of the multiplication of numbers inherent in economic and social modernization.

In the short run of a generation or two, optimism concerning a reduction of the pressures of population increase requires an intensive rationality among the illiterate peasants of a familistic society. Under the conditions of the past, any planning that involved low fertility in Chinese villages would have seemed quite unrealistic. But in that past, the belief that any government of China could or would adopt and implement campaigns to reduce fertility in the villages would have seemed quite unrealistic.

The future of Mainland China's population has to be assessed in the context of a state in revolution and a society in disruption. The driving ideological goals of the Communist state include the destruction of all those institutions of the old order that are labeled as feudalistic. The family system and the Confucian ethic must be dethroned, for otherwise the Communists will follow all China's other conquerors—perverted by or absorbed into the society they have seemingly conquered. Personal freedom in marriage, the equality of women, the liquidation of the gentry—these are the essential bases for the creation of the Communist order. They are also the processes of social change that may permit a swift indoctrination of limited childbearing as a phase of the new life and the new party orthodoxy. This is speculative, but there is no approach other than speculation to a future for which history has no precedent.

The assault on the birth rate is but one aspect, even a minor aspect, of the activities that influence the productive capacity of the economy of China and the characteristics and attitudes of the people. Industrialization, increased food production, and the development of the frontier areas involve not alone the capacity to feed more people but the change from rural to urban living for increasing proportions of the people. Mass education and the incessant study activities that carry the indoctrination to local levels may transform codes and behavior in the village society. The fundamental assault is on Chinese culture itself rather than on the high birth rate.

The future course of the population of China may seem to be a dependent variable, and in many ways it is. But given the immensity of the Chinese population and the formidable barriers to economic development, the rate of increase of the population may become the most critical of all the factors of change. If the Communists do not so recognize it at present, it is likely that they will be forced to do so eventually. The approach to population policy in recent months is only a prelude to the government program that may be anticipated in the future.

3

THE FAMILY IN CHINA,
PAST AND PRESENT

Maurice Freedman

The western literature on which we draw for much of our knowledge of the family in China is full of variations on the theme that
the family was the basic unit of Chinese society. In one sense the
statement must certainly be true. In any society the family is the
group which produces the personnel to man the wider institutions;
and in the process of generating social beings it impresses on them
certain principles of conduct which have a bearing on the way in
which they discharge their general tasks. The family is therefore
basic. But this is not significantly truer of China than of most other
societies, and what people usually appear to mean when they assert
that the family was the basic unit of Chinese society is one of two
things: either that the family provided the model for the society
as a whole, such that even the total polity might be regarded as one
massive family, or that family relationships predominated in their
potency over all other kinds of relationship.

There are both naïve and sophisticated versions of these views.
A simple-minded account of China treats the emperor as the patriarch of a blown-up family formed by the empire as a whole. On
this view it is possible to ascribe to the Chinese polity a benign
authoritarianism exercised over a mass of patient and pious children by a stern yet considerate father. In more technical discussions
the dominance of Chinese society by the family is expressed by as-

Dr. Freedman, Reader in Anthropology, The London School of Economics and Political Science, is the author of *Lineage Organization in
Southeastern China* (1958). This article is reprinted with permission
from *Pacific Affairs*, Vol. 34, No. 4 (Winter 1961-1962), 323-336. Copyright
© 1962 by the University of British Columbia. The concluding paragraphs, which are a call for intensified research on the Chinese family,
have been omitted.

signing to it a strength which inhibits men in their dealings—say, their economic transactions—with members of other families.

Behind the confusion lies a failure, in the first place, to distinguish between family as a specific social group on the one hand and kinship on the other. We can show without much difficulty that kinship bound together large numbers of people in Chinese society and exerted an important effect on their political, economic, and religious conduct at large. Family is another matter. Essentially, its realm is that of domestic life, a realm of coresidence and the constant involvement in affairs of the hearth, children, and marriage. Kinship is something different. Outside his family a Chinese was bound by rights and duties to people related to him through ties of descent and marriage. The relationships traced exclusively through males, as a special set of kinship relations, might be so extensive and organized as to form patrilineal descent groups. These groups are often referred to in the literature as clans, but it is becoming more common nowadays to give them the technically more satisfactory name of lineages.

Localized lineages were in some parts of the country (especially in the southeast) so wide in their extent that they encompassed large villages and sometimes even towns. Almost inevitably, some of their members were rich and others poor. Some might well be scholars, others illiterate. Some could move with ease in the wider political society; others were simple countrymen, deprived of influence. Yet lineages are sometimes represented as though they were families. People who make the mistake of thinking of them in this fashion may well be puzzled by the unfamily-like behavior shown by, say, a rich man squeezing his debtor-kinsman or an elder forcing his kinsman-inferior to pay him the deference due to one standing high in the general system of status of the society. A lineage is no family.

But let us assume that the problem is to decide what strength or potency lay in kinship relations as a whole. We may take China as it was in the last hundred years of its existence as an imperial state. The question resolves itself into an analysis of how the solidarities and values of kinship were enmeshed in a political and economic order which required of individuals that they owe allegiance to a state and participate, despite the dominance of agriculture, in a wide-ranging economic system.

From the point of view of the state, a man's obligations to it were in fact both qualified and mediated by his kinship relations. They were qualified in the sense that obligations springing from filial piety and mourning duties were held to modify duties owed to the state. An official who lost a parent was supposed to retire during his mourning. People related to one another in close bonds of kinship were so far regarded by the written law to require solidarity among them that the Code provided that certain relatives might legitimately conceal the offenses of one another (except in cases of high treason and rebellion), either escaping punishment altogether or suffering a penalty reduced in accordance with the closeness of the relationship; and that it was an offense generally for close kinsmen to lay even just accusations against one another. There was built into the system the principle that close patrilineal kinship set up special rights and duties standing apart from the rights and duties between man and the state. The structure of these privileged rights was conceived in terms of mourning duties, the relations between two kinsmen being expressed as a function of the mourning ritual due between them. For this reason the Code specified the grades and duration of mourning and the ritual costume associated with them.

In the eyes of the state, then, a man stood posed against it in a network of primary kinship duties. But the state also regarded kinship units as part of its system of general control, so that a man's duties to it were mediated through his membership of these units. The family is the clearest case. The Confucian emphasis on complex families and the legal power vested in the head of a family to prevent its premature breakup are aspects of a total political system in which some authority is delegated from the administrative system to what, in a metaphorical sense, we may call natural units. The Confucian moralizing about the family, the stress put upon filial piety and the need for solidarity among brothers, the underlining of the importance of domestic harmony—these reflect a political view in which units standing at the base of the social pyramid are expected to control themselves in the interest of the state.

But the family is not the only case. It was morally right for men to align themselves on the basis of their common patrilineal descent and to form lineages. Lineage organization implied ancestor worship, a Confucian value of high order. It implied the promotion of schools and mutual help; in these the state could take pleasure. It implied, finally, an organization which could be used by the state for political and fiscal control. And at once we can see the dilemma faced by the state when it tried to make use of the lineage and encourage its prosperity. To be of use to the state the lineage must be organized and strong; but strength might grow to the point at which what was once a useful adjunct of government now became a threat to it. Where the lineages grew in numbers and riches, they fought with other lineages. This was objectionable enough, but clearly what frightened the central administration more than anything else was the tendency for patrilineal organization to snowball. A lineage was justified by a genealogy; people began to produce longer and wider genealogies to justify more extensive groupings, going so far—and this "excess" excited very great official indignation—that attempts were sometimes made to group together in one organization all the lineages in one area bearing a common surname. It is important to realize that genealogical rearrangement and the grouping together of lineages make perfect sense given the logic of the patrilineal system, and that the objections raised by officialdom, although they might be couched in terms condemning the falsification of genealogies, were essentially political. That is to say, strong nuclei of local power were being created which constituted a threat to state authority.

From the political point of view, then, kinship organization entailed a balance of forces with the state. By incorporating in its ideals a high value set upon family and kinship and by attempting to make use of their institutions, the state involved itself in a struggle to keep them in check. Indeed, one aspect of a political system which might appear to be arbitrary and oppressive is that it called into being forces which negated its tendencies to be just that.

On the role of kinship in economic life we have no systematic and large body of information on which to rely, but we can make a general argument. If we start from the assumption that kinship relations and values predominate in the conduct of economic affairs, we must expect that enterprise will take the form of what is often called the family business. Now, of course, there is plenty of evidence to show that Chinese economic enterprise has tended strongly to be organized so that people associating their capital, or capital and labor, are related by kinship or affinity. But what is the real significance of this fact? Is it that the moral imperatives of kinship impel people to seek out kinsmen with whom to work? The answer is no. Given the nature of the capital market, given a legal system which offers little protection to business, given the tendency to rely on people with whom there is some preceding tie, we should expect that kinsmen would be associating with one another in economic activities. What is really involved is that these activities are made to rest on highly personalized relationships and that a man's circle of relatives is likely to contain the greater number of individuals apt for selection. It is important to remember that, outside the family, a kinsman has few specific economic claims, that he can be approached as a landlord or creditor as any other landlord or creditor, and that in general we must not look to see preference being shown to a kinsman in economic matters on the grounds simply that he is a kinsman.

We have so far been concerned with the question of how far the family in "premodern" China can be said to have been the basic unit of society. The argument has taken the form that family and kinship together provided one method of balancing the power of the state and that kinship was not *in principle* basic to economic life. If we confined our attention to the family in the strictest sense of the term, we might be able, by noting how much of the ordinary individual's life is lived within it, to assert that we were dealing with something fundamental. But in doing this we should be ignoring the whole range of wider institutions without which the family can in fact have little meaning.

We must now turn to the inner structure of the Chinese family before modern times, placing emphasis on two things: first, the nature of the tensions inherent in it, in order to see whether they can help us in our understanding of modern developments; and second, the linkages between the family and the wider society, so that we may look for changes in the family which may correspond to changes in society at large.

The experts have been insisting for the last twenty years that it is incorrect to say that the Chinese family in traditional circumstances was big. We need not, therefore, put much stress on the fact that average size of the family was five or six persons, but rather consider why it was that some families were very large and others very small, with many gradations between these extremes. Let us go back to the political point that the state looked to the family as the first unit of social control. The ideal family from this point of view was one in which large numbers of kinsmen and their wives were held under the control of a patriarch imbued with the Confucian values of propriety and order. Some families came close to this model, several generations living under one roof. They were powerful families. We may consider the power they wielded in terms both of their control of economic resources and of their command over other people. They were rich. They owned much land and other capital resources. By renting land and lending money they could exert influence over other people. They could afford to educate their sons and equip them for membership of the bureaucratic elite. They often (perhaps usually) entered into the life of this elite, making use of their ties in it to control both less fortunate families and their own subordinate members. Such a family may be looked upon as a large politico-economic corporation with much power vested in its chief member. But this corporation could not grow indefinitely in membership, for with the death of its senior generation it split along the lines laid down by the constitution of the next generation, every son having a right to an individualized share of his father's estate on that man's death. However, despite the partition which took place every generation, high status families were able to remain large. The passing of the senior generation was likely to take place at a point when the men in the next generation were themselves old enough to have descendants sufficient for complex families of their own. At this level of society fertility was relatively high, the chances of survival were higher, adoption was easy, the age of marriage was low, and plural marriage was possible.

At the other end of the social scale the family was, so to speak, scarcely Confucian. Poverty and powerlessness produced, instead of a strong patriarch, a weak father. He could rally no support from outside to dominate his sons. He had few resources to withhold from them. In fact, he might well have only one son growing to maturity. If, however, he had two or more sons reaching manhood, only one would be likely to stay with him, and perhaps even this one would leave him too. Demography, economics, and the power situation at this level of society ensured that families of simple structure were a constant feature of the landscape.

Changes in social status promoted changes in family structure. Upward social mobility was partly a matter of increasing the complexity of the family, both because changing demographic, economic, and power conditions entailed complexity and because the ideal Confucian family was a model towards which people strove when they were moving upwards. And we should note that downward social mobility brought with it a corresponding decline in complexity.

The relations between the sexes and between the generations were dependent on differences in family structure. It will be convenient to start from a feature of Chinese family life which has always attracted the attention of outsiders: the unhappy position of the daughter-in-law. She may be looked upon from three points of view: as a woman, as a member of the family by incorporation, and as a member of a junior generation. It needs no stressing that being a woman was a disadvantage. Every aspect of her society and its values left the Chinese woman in no doubt on that score. In the family into which she was born she might indeed be well and affectionately treated, but this favorable treatment rested on the paradox that she was merely a temporary member of it. Certainly, her marriage would call upon the family's resources, for it would cause her father to assert his status by sending her off in such a manner as to narrow the status gap between him and the father of the groom. But her marriage cut her off economically and as a legal person from her own family and transferred the rights in and over her to the family receiving her. In this new family she was at once a stranger and a member—the former because she was new and the latter in that, henceforth, the rights and duties in respect of her would lie with her husband's people. From the day of her marriage she must begin to think of her interests as being inevitably involved in those of her husband and the members of his family. She had no secure base outside this family from which to operate, because, while she might try to bring in support from her family of birth to moderate oppression, she could not rely on it. To a large extent physically and in all degrees legally, she was locked within her husband's gates.

Her husband's mother was her point of contact with the new senior generation to preside over her—whence her tears, for she had to be disciplined into a new role in a new family. In fact, however, the difficulties faced by the daughter-in-law were only one aspect of a broader configuration of difficulties. Men in Confucian morality were urged to reject the claims made by their wives on their attention and their interests, and to stand by their brothers against the threat posed to fraternal solidarity by their wives. Women were troublemakers, partly because they were strangers. Her mother-in-law represented for the wife the female half of the family into which she was firmly thrust if her husband refused to come to her aid. Mother-in-law, daughters-in-law, and unmarried daughters formed a battlefield on which any one daughter-in-law must fight for herself and, later, for her children.

Now if in fact the married brothers in a family did stand together, refusing to listen to their wives' complaints, it was because

they were posed against their father. And this father was a strong
figure whose power rested on the economic resources he controlled
and the command he could exert on the world outside the family.
It will be seen, therefore, that we have been dealing with the characteristics of a family of high status. Because of riches, life might
in one sense be easy for the married woman (she had servants and
other luxuries), but she was distant from her husband and at the
mercy of the other women in the house until she was herself senior
enough to pass from the dominated to the dominators.

In a family of low status and simple structure the elemental relationships of father and son, brother and brother, and husband
and wife formed a different pattern. The father's control was weak
and the brothers were highly individualized among themselves.
Each brother stood close to his wife, so that while the wife might
be made miserable by poverty and hard work, at the lower levels
of society she had greater strength as an individual. Here she was
far less likely to need to cope with other mature women in the
house.

From this summary analysis we may conclude that the probability of tension between the generations and the sexes increased with
a rise in social status, and we may look forward from this point to
the attempts made in modern times to remedy what seemed to be
the difficulties and injustices of the Chinese family system.

In the years following the 1911 Revolution, changes in ideas and
law reflected a lively preoccupation among intellectuals with problems of family reform. Let us take a single example, chosen partly
because of the way in which sociology is called in to support reformist arguments. In a paper written in 1928, Quentin Pan, who
at this period was much concerned with problems of this sort, proposed a basic reform in terms of the "optimum family." In such a
family the women, as in tradition, would be sent out on marriage,
but "any male will have to start a family of his own as soon as he
marries and is able to be self-supporting." When there was more
than one son "the parents may live with each in turn at allotted
intervals." In other words, the brothers should divide while making
provision for the maintenance of the tie between the generations.
"The 'greater family,'" Pan goes on, "is obviously a sociological
mistake." It is numerically unwieldy, it suppresses individualism,
and leads to psychological difficulty and discord. "If the greater
family is a sociological blunder, the smaller one is a biological one."
That is to say, the complete rejection by married sons of their par-

ents means a lack of reciprocity between the generations; those who are cared for in childhood do not care later on for their parents. "Suffer your aged parents to stay with you and your children so that there will be constant association and interchange of sentiments. . . ." In effect Pan proposes that each complex family should give way to a series of elementary families (married couples and their children) and a "stem" family in which the old people would be living with one of their married sons.

In its naïve way this statement makes an analysis of the problems inherent in the high-status family. What is more interesting, it puts forward a remedy which was in fact represented in reality by the family system of the greater part of the population, for whom the unwieldy family suppressing individualism was ruled out by poverty and lack of power.

The intellectual urge to reform was not, needless to say, inspired by inspection of the advantages enjoyed in family life by the lower orders. It stemmed in large measure from Western notions of modernity and progress. Somehow family institutions were to be reshaped to fit an imminently new form of society. One way of procuring this end was to legislate for it. After many years of debate a Civil Code dealing with many aspects of family life was in 1931 put on the statute book. One may well question the seriousness of the Code as a political attempt at social reform, but even if we regard it in much the same light as its imperial predecessor—that is to say, as a general statement of models of behavior rather than a body of detailed rules to be closely applied—it is still important because of the ideological investment made in it by the intellectuals of the day (many of whom looked upon it as a beacon of light) and because of the nature of the sociological insight employed in its construction. In fact, the Code turned out to be far less revolutionary than a superficial impression would convey. As scholars have pointed out, the provisions of the Code are rather conservative in the compromise reached between the needs of tradition and the call for modernism. Yet, for all its conservatism, it marked a major step in Chinese history. Before it was produced, the republican courts were still bound by rules springing from the old order and might be forced to give recognition to practises likely to raise eyebrows in the world at large. In 1919, for example, in a case arising from a man's selling his wife, the Supreme Court ruled that the "purchase of a woman for the explicit purpose of begetting children is justifiable and not invalid."

The new Code's provisions have accumulated around them a considerable literature of scholarship, and there would be no point in trying to spell out details here. Broadly, the woman as child and wife acquires an enhanced status in the crucial spheres of property, marriage, and divorce, such that her rights are made more symmetrical with those of a man. Monogamy is established, but it is a monogamy which, given the tacit consent of the wife, allows a man to set up permanent relationships with other women from which legally recognized children may issue. The Code assumes an essentially patrilineal and patriarchal family, but it restricts the rights exerted over immature children and asserts the rights of mature children to go their own way. Yet rights to maintenance from children and grandchildren are written into the law. In effect, we have a set of rules which in many respects support the kind of family system envisaged as ideal by Quentin Pan: Patriliny is preserved, but the ground is cut away from beneath the complex domestic unit.

The patrilineal configuration of rights and duties in traditional law is changed in the Civil Code into a system of reckoning kinship according to the Roman Law system. Yet in both Civil and Penal Codes something remains of the traditional solidarities expected among close kinsmen. The old absolute prohibition of marriage within the patrilineal *wu fu* (that is, with all cousins bearing the same surname closer than fourth) reappears, although obscured by the new legal language. In the Penal Code the "penalties for maltreatment, for unlawful confinement, false accusation, and murder are heavier when these offenses are committed against parents, grandparents, or great grandparents. . . . The penalty for theft from relatives having joint property and living in the same house can be suspended, and no one can be prosecuted for theft from relatives within the fifth degree of relationship (by blood) and within the third degree by marriage without the victim's complaint. . . ." In other words, we are still in a Chinese world where reform has not yet tried to destroy, even at the symbolic level of the law, some of the most fundamental principles of cohesion in the family and among close kinsmen. In the eyes of the state the family continues to be an essential element of the total social and political order.

When we turn to the new state established in Mainland China since 1949, we may begin by making the opposite assumption. The family is to be destroyed. How far will this take us in understand-

ing what is afoot in Communist China? We may start by looking
at the Marriage Law of the People's Republic, for this, despite its
narrow title, constitutes a code for the regulation of family matters,
and we may safely assume that it represents a far more serious attempt to change society than its Nationalist predecessor, at least by
virtue of the positiveness with which it is applied. It is couched in
very general and vague language, and its exact import in regard to
particular matters could be gauged only from a study of the cases
to which it has given rise. Yet the essential purposes to which it is
directed are very clear. Marriage is to be a free contract between
individuals, and one which, in the last resort, may be broken at the
will of one party. The family vanishes as a party to marriage. An
almost perfect symmetry of the rights of men and women is erected
—in property, residence, choice of work, and control of children.
Indeed, one might argue that the new law is concerned basically
with only one question: the procreating, raising, and care of children.

There are, however, two features of the new rules which speak
for the legal survival of tradition. The first is a clause which adds
a prohibition to the bar on marriage between lineal kinsmen and
between brothers and sisters: "The question of prohibiting marriage between collateral relatives by blood within the fifth degree
of relationship is to be determined by custom." We are back to the
patrilineal *wu fu* and provided with some evidence that society is
not to be remodeled, at least not for the present, in every minute
detail. The second aspect of traditionalism lies in the treatment of
the duties of children towards their parents. "Parents have the duty
to rear and educate their children; the children have the duty to
look after and assist their parents. . . . Neither the parents nor
the children shall maltreat or desert one another. . . . Parents and
children shall have the right to inherit one another's property."
Something of the old system is to be left.

But what does the remnant amount to? The concession to custom
in the marriage prohibitions is a temporary affair. Given the nature
of the Communist economy, what property claims on children
would be important? Given the political nature of the new state,
what is likely to amount to a child's desertion of his parents? Our
initial assumption that the family is to be destroyed seems to be
borne out. The old kinship system, which elaborated patriliny into
corporate units of social structure, has been washed away. There is
no room in a Communist polity for such nuclei of power. Devolu-

tion of power there must be in any political system, however tyrannical, but it cannot be reposed in units which by their very nature may turn it against those who have conceded it. The Communist rulers of China are not likely to fall into the dilemma of their imperial predecessors, who from time to time were embarrassed by the resistance set up in areas of society which they themselves supported by their Confucian regard for kinship values. From land reform to the establishment of the communes the society has passed through a process in which principles of local aggregation and leadership have been thoroughly made over. Even if in terms of population a lineage still occupies the same area, its erstwhile leaders now lack the economic resources and power, the ritual authority, and the external political support and connections to allow them to continue to have meaning. And beyond the range of the single lineage, the lateral bonds of clanship—uniting lineages in their common interest—are broken by the lack of ritual centers and the confinement of social relations within units laid down by the state for the benefit of its system of control.

China is now more bureaucratic than ever before. In the old days bureaucracy was checked both because its officers stopped at the county seat and because ambiguous loyalty was institutionalized. Up to a point a man was expected to work against the interests of the state in the cause of his kinsmen. Even as it tried to check nepotism, the state promoted it. But the new bureaucracy works on a purer model. Loyalty must have but one focus. Bureaucratic influence must reach down right into the affairs of the smallest units of society. Certainly, children must respect their parents, but a parent disloyal to the state must run the risk of seeing his child cast his own loyalty to the state against that to his parent.

The family now lies open to the state. It has little property to hold it together. Its ritual bond has been removed. Its head can call on few sanctions to support him in the exercise of authority—his wife can divorce him, his children defy him. The allocation of tasks in economic life is not now in any important respect a family matter. The whole range of activities once covered by the family is now reduced to a narrow field in which husband, wife, and children associate together in the interstices, so to speak, of large institutions—the work group, the dining hall, the nursery—which have taken over the functions of economic coordination, housekeeping, and the rearing and education of children. The family has become an institution for producing babies and enjoying the leisure time left over from the major pursuits of everyday life.

Now, as soon as we formulate our account of the contemporary Chinese family in this fashion—and, of course, the account may well be overdrawn, which in fact strengthens the argument to follow—we can no longer rely on the assumption that the family is to be destroyed. The more we look at this picture, the more familiar it will seem to us, for it contains features from the Western experience of family life. For most of the inhabitants of an industrialized society the family is a small residential group from which many of the major activities of life are excluded. The factory, the office, and the school separate the members of one family for many hours of the day and provide them with different ranges of relationships and interests. What they unite for as a family is a restricted number of activities of consumption, child care, amusement, and emotional exchange. True, if we are to believe what we are told, the Chinese family in the commune has gone further in reducing the minimal functions we associate with family life, but it has not necessarily departed in principle from a pattern which we know to be intrinsic to the modern form of society.

If we begin a discussion of whether the family now exists in China with a definition of the family which lists a number of functions, it is possible that we shall deny it to present-day China, just as some people have denied it to collective settlements in Israel. If instead we look in the family for a configuration of relationships between spouses and between parents and children, a configuration standing out from the other patterns of relationship in which people are involved, then we should have little difficulty in satisfying ourselves that the Chinese family has survived.

But there is more to it than that. We can argue that the family has survived not *against* the wishes of the people responsible for policy in Communist China but rather in accordance with their desire to see the institution persist and flourish. The persistence is, of course, on their terms, but what they may seek to perpetuate is necessary for the orderly working of their society. Marriage may be potentially fragile, but marriage there certainly is. Its purpose is to provide a locus for the raising of useful citizens. Children are not going to be produced on an assembly line; they must be linked to parents before they can be linked to society. In the early years of their control the Communists gave the appearance of waging a war

on the family. Since about 1953, the war having been won to their
satisfaction, they have been at pains to stress such of the values of
family life as they regard as important in the institution as it now
is. Old people must be looked after by their children; the young
must be respectful; there must be a harmonious relationship between husband and wife.

It would appear that the form taken by the family in recent years
is essentially the same as that which we have seen to have characterized the greater part of the Chinese population before any of
the modern trends began. That is to say, the family is either a unit
of parents and their immature children, or it includes in addition
to these people the parents or surviving parent of the husband or
the wife (of the former rather than of the latter). The "solution"
produced by the Communists is in reality an old one, and in arriv-
ing at it the Communists were continuing a process of change which
had started many years earlier at the higher levels of Chinese society. In fact, it could be argued that just as the Communists worked
on peasant hunger for land to bind the mass of the people to them
in the early days of land reform, so they commanded the allegiance
of many people by playing on the stresses inherent in complex
family organization. The resentment of the wife and the son, and
the strains between the sexes and the generations were material on
which politics could work to create opinion favorable to its general
aims. The Communists made Quentin Pan's "optimum family" universal; it brought them allies. They fulfilled the ambitions of the
Westernizing intellectuals even while damning what they were attacking as "feudal" and "bourgeois."

4

CHINESE AGRICULTURE

John Lossing Buck

Chinese agriculture is almost as different from European agriculture as is Chinese civilization from European civilization. The technique of crop and animal production, however, is practically the same in both civilizations, except for contrasts in the extent of the development of agricultural science. It is rather the type of land utilization and the success in land use that differentiates the agriculture of the Oriental and the Western civilizations. . . .

The topography of China varies from great plains at nearly sea level to very rough mountainous country at elevations over 10,000 feet—so high as to be above the limit of crop production, and is one of the very important factors responsible for the type of land use in many sections. For instance, in the northwest the elevation becomes so high as to shorten the growing season so that only crops such as oats, Irish potatoes, and proso-millet can be grown. On the other hand, in the same latitude on the great plains at nearly sea level such crops as cotton, peanuts, and corn are grown with success, and much of the land even produces two crops in one year. Fortunately, most of the agricultural land is at the lower elevations, which make large agricultural production possible.

The climate of China is very diverse. Latitude, altitude, winter and summer monsoons, cyclonic storms, and typhoons—all have a

For many years before and during World War II, Dr. Buck was Professor of Agricultural Economics at the University of Nanking, where under his direction pioneer field studies of the Chinese farm economy were carried out. The present selection is reprinted from Chapter 1 of the first volume of his monumental work *Land Utilization in China* (University of Nanking, 1937), with the permission of the United Board for Christian Higher Education in Asia and The Council on Economic and Cultural Affairs, Inc. Some deletions have been made in the text.

part in determining the climate in any one section. Winter monsoons give north China her cold, dry, sunny winters, while the summer monsoons are chiefly relied upon for the rainfall required for crop production. Typhoons which accompany the summer monsoons help to cool the air and ameliorate the oppressive summers of southern China. Precipitation decreases from the southeast to the northwest and varies from 85 to only 13 inches, or even less, if one includes the desert portions which are outside the scope of this study. Precipitation is least dependable in north China, where it is the lowest and where over 80 per cent of it falls in the summer months. Much of the summer rainfall throughout China is of the convectional type, and thus much of its utility is lost because of excessive runoff. Evaporation is increased by the high winds of north China, and thus it is that the effectiveness of the low rainfall for growth is greatly reduced. The great variability of precipitation is responsible for floods or drought, with consequent famines.

Temperatures also increase from the northwest to the southwest, from a January mean of 12°F. to one of 57°F. and a July mean of 73°F. to 84°F. The growing season ranges from the full year in the south to one of less than 130 days in the northwest, and the type of crops grown are affected accordingly—oranges in the south; and oats, spring wheat, and Irish potatoes (typical of the sections with a short growing season) in the northwest.

The humidity of south China is favorable for tea but unfavorable for cotton, especially at harvest time. Sunshine is required for the satisfactory maturing of cotton and wheat; and thus north China with its sunshine in the late spring and early autumn is favorable to both of these crops. The winds of north China cause dust storms in late winter and spring, which work havoc with crops in addition to creating an unfavorable environment for human life. A hot May wind may reduce the wheat crop greatly by "blighting." Strong winds in south China at rice-blossom time often curtail the rice production. Hail limits crop production, particularly in the northwest. . . .

The nature of the soils in any country depends to a large extent upon climatic factors. North China, with its meager rainfall, has an unleached calcium soil (Pedocal soil) while south China, with abundant rain, has a leached or acid soil (Pedalfer soil). Transported soils comprise about nine tenths of the agricultural soils of China. The vast loessial or wind-blown soils of the northwest, and the alluvial deposits of the Yellow, Yangtze, and other rivers of east and south China make up the larger portion of these transported soils. The other one tenth are residual soils, found usually on hills and mountains as a result of disintegration and weathering of rocks. As a whole, the residual soils are less fertile than the transported ones, and in many cases are extremely infertile.

There are many soil groups of varying fertility within the two categories of leached and unleached soils. The unleached or slightly leached soils are fairly rich in mineral constituents suitable for plant food but are deficient in organic matter, partly because of the burning of crop residue for fuel—even to the pulling up of the roots of crops for this purpose. Scarcity of rainfall, however, is the chief factor limiting the productivity of these soils.

The leached soils have had much of the mineral plant foods reduced below the point of availability to the plant. Moreover, rapid oxidation makes constant additions of large quantities of organic matter necessary. Fertilization is, therefore, even more important in south China than in north China. . . .

Crop insects, pests, and diseases seem more prevalent in China than in many other countries. There is little scientific control, and for this reason they flourish and limit production probably by as much as 10 to 20 per cent of the crop. Aphis, smuts, rusts, locusts, boll worms, and grubs are among the most prevalent of these plant enemies. Animal diseases are also important, especially rinderpest among cattle. Many of these losses are preventable at small cost, and such control is one of the easiest ways of increasing production. . . .

Access to markets, or what might be termed geographical location, and transportation facilities affect the type of crop production. Bulky products of small value per unit of weight cannot be shipped long distances. China is a country of great distances; and this, combined with primitive methods of transportation—such as carrying goods by a pole over the shoulder and, to a lesser extent, by cart and junk—makes distance from the market an important factor in determining the type of production. The methods of transportation used make it possible to carry goods from 40 to 300 miles at costs of 1.62 yuan by carrying by a pole over the shoulder, and 0.39 yuan by junk. Rail and steamboat transportation is increasing, but still the predominant methods are the more laborious and inefficient ones. Moreover, unimproved roads limit the efficiency of the present systems of transportation and limit the time of marketing. For instance, in the absence of a well-developed transportation system opium has become a crop particularly adapted to the frontier provinces; and crops are produced on mountain sides better adapted to forests, because of the inaccessibility of markets. Thus, not only is the type of agricultural crop grown affected, but even the type of land use as between forests and agriculture.

It is now clear that certain basic factors limit the type of agriculture possible in various sections of China. The next step is to discover the type of land use developed under the limits set by these conditions.

Within an approximate total gross area of some 1,400,000 square miles, in agricultural China—exclusive of the three northeastern provinces—340,000 square miles, or approximately one fourth, is cultivated. This amount compares favorably with other countries with percentages of land area cultivated varying from 12 to 45 per cent. The other three fourths of the gross area not cultivated has a little over one half in some kind of productive use—chiefly in trees, grass, and reeds for fuel—but over one fifth is in forest and 12 per cent in pasture. The arable portion of this uncultivated land is estimated to be over one tenth, but that estimate does not give sufficient consideration to the profitability of cultivating such land or to the length of time it can be cultivated with profit. Much of this supposedly arable land has had the topsoil washed away by sheet erosion and is therefore difficult to bring into profitable production. The development of better transportation facilities and cheaper supplies of fertilizer will increase the amount of this land which may be brought into cultivation with profit.

Of all land, 27 per cent is utilized for crops, 4.6 per cent for pasture, 8.7 per cent for forest, and the remaining 59.7 per cent is for other purposes or is valueless.

Land in farms (farm area) is used to approximately 90 per cent in crops; nearly four per cent in roads, ponds, graves, and the like; over three per cent in farmsteads; over one per cent in pasture land and wooded pasture; one per cent in forest; over one half of one per cent in grass and bushes cut for fuel; and three tenths of one per cent in ponds producing water crops or fish. Ninety per cent of the farm area of China is in crops—compared with 42 per cent in the United States. On the other hand, pasture in China constitutes only 1.1 per cent of the farm area, as compared with 47 per cent of the area in the United States. Herein is the great contrast between Chinese and American or Western agriculture. It denotes a small animal industry in China and a consequent low food consumption of animal products, as compared with a large animal industry and a high consumption of animal products in many of the Western countries. Early Chinese civilization shows no evidence of use of animal products to a greater extent than at present. It is the use of vegetarian products that has made possible a density of 1,500 farm population per square mile of cultivated land. Whether or not this represents a more efficient use of land will be discussed later. It is an intensive type of land use, even to the point of developing water areas for such crops as water chestnut and for fish culture. In south China a large portion of the farms have at least one pond for such purposes.

In China, man has greatly modified the land for farming purposes. Nearly one half is irrigated chiefly for rice, although irrigation is common in many sections of north China. Water is pumped chiefly by means of human power, although animal pumps are quite common and windmills less frequently found. Recently the oil engine has been successfully introduced on a commercial basis in the lower Yangtze valley. The sources of water are streams, ponds, canals, lagoons, or wells, the latter being chiefly confined to the large plains of north China. Irrigation involves not only application of water to the land but in the Rice Region, especially, it entails the leveling of land so that the fields can be maintained in a flooded condition. It also concerns human relations, since economic organization is required for successful irrigation projects. Many a village quarrel over irrigation water not infrequently becomes a battle waged with hoes and other agricultural implements. Water rights in China still need to be more clearly defined and upheld by means of proper laws justly enforced.

What constitutes terracing of land is subject to definition, but it is estimated that one quarter of all the cultivated land is so modified, not only to hold water for rice culture in south China, but to make cultivation easier, to prevent erosion, and in parts of north China to catch surface runoff where the terraced fields are not irrigated. Except for the very level land of south China, all rice fields may be said to be terraced, although the term is usually thought of in relation to the more pronounced terraces of the hillsides. . . .

Soils of China are modified by fertilization as in most other countries. In China, however, three practices exist in addition to the use of farm manures universally applied throughout the world. Human excrement is used throughout China—in south China in liquid form with urine and feces applied directly on the growing crop, while in north China only the dried feces are used and applied directly to the soil. The application of such "night soil" in liquid form is one of the great menaces to health, as many intestinal diseases are transmitted through the bare feet of farmers working in such fields. Raw vegetables cannot be safely eaten because of this practice, but when properly cooked such vegetables are as safe and wholesome as the drinking water of modern cities in the West, which is so often obtained from rivers in which sewers of cities are emptied.

Oil cakes, the residue from expressing oil from seeds of soybeans, sesame, cotton, rapeseed, tea oil nuts, and wood oil nuts, are extensively used for direct fertilization. If these cakes were first fed to animals, 80 per cent of their fertilizing value would still be returned to the land in animal manures—a practice which would probably be an improvement in farm economy over the present one.

Ashes from byproducts of crops—straw and stalks—and from grass and bushes cut from the hills, burned for cooking and heating purposes, are used as fertilizer throughout the country and supply considerable potash to the soils. This practice also is a doubtful one in farm economy because much of these byproducts could be utilized for feeding animals, and the fertility returned in animal manures.

Much of the soil erosion found in China is essentially a form of modification by man with the help of nature. Man has cut the forests or broken up grasslands and has neglected to protect the soil thus exposed from being slowly or even rapidly washed away. Consequently, vast quantities of topsoil have been wasted by sheet erosion and even still larger quantities by gully erosion. One needs only to observe the sea of gulleys in the loessial highlands of the northwest and the heavily laden muddy waters of these rivers extending far out into the sea, or to realize the rate with which the Yangtze river is building up the coast of the province of Kiangsu, to realize that the upland soils of China are being rapidly destroyed. In some places where this destruction is slow, the soil building processes may keep pace with it, but there is a net loss which probably limits agricultural production as much as it can be increased through any improvement adopted, such as better fertilization, improved seeds, and control of insects and plant diseases.

In China, modification of land by man has taken place to a much greater degree than in a new and less densely populated country like the United States. The combination of cheap labor and high land values means that land which in other countries might be marginal for farming, or used for forest or for pasture, can be used for farming purposes in China.

Land in China is almost entirely privately owned, there being only seven per cent held by the State. This privately owned land is mostly in the hands of individuals, but a small portion, less than one per cent, is owned by temples and family clans and leased to tenants. Somewhat less than three fourths of the privately owned farm land is owned by the farmer himself, and over one fourth is rented. Owner farms are larger than tenant farms, averaging 4.22 acres as compared with 3.56 acres. Consequently, a little over one half of the farmers are owners, less than one third part owners, and 17 per cent are tenants. Farmers who own their farmsteads but who rent all their crop land are classified as tenants rather than as part owners. Tenancy is much more prevalent in south China than in north China and varies greatly in amount for different sections of the country, from no tenants to all farmers as tenants. . . .

Fragmentation of land—the ownership by individuals of scattered pieces of land—is the rule in China. The number of such pieces per landholding is unknown, but there are nearly six pieces (or parcels) per farm, averaging a little less than an acre in size. Such fragmentation has the disadvantages of using up land in boundaries, increasing the number of boundary disputes, consuming time to reach the plots, increasing the difficulties of irrigation, limiting the size of fields and hence the use of machinery, and making crop protection difficult. The chief advantage is that one farmer may have land of differing qualities, and this is important in a country of small farms where a complete crop failure would be disastrous.

The unfenced fields are nearly twelve per farm of not quite one half an acre each. The fields are too small for much farm machinery; but the limiting factor in the use of such machinery is not in the main the smallness of fields or farms as such, but in a dense population which makes labor cheap and the use of machinery uneconomical.

Graves in China are placed to a large extent in the farmer's fields, in spots determined as desirable by the geomancer, regardless of their hindrance to farm operations. Such graves occupy almost two per cent of all farm land in China. A more intensive use of land in China could be brought about by the removal of graves from farm land, by the elimination of land in boundaries, by consolidation of fragmented holdings, by the profitable cultivation of arable lands not now cultivated, and by an economic unit size of farm which would lessen the proportion of area in farmsteads. This might make available nearly another twenty-five million acres for the eight agricultural areas of China.

The kind of crops grown on nine tenths of the farm land of China is another criterion of the type of land use. Those crops which appear as the most important in the type of farming for China as a whole are rice and wheat for food, and cotton for clothing and other textile uses. Other crops characteristic for the country as a whole, occupying one per cent or more of the crop acreage, in order of importance, are: millet, soybeans, kaoliang, barley, corn, sweet potatoes, rapeseed, broad beans, peanuts, *astragalus sinensis* for green manure, green beans (*mung* bean), field peas, and the opium poppy. The mulberry tree (grown for its leaves for the silkworm), tea, oranges, and tobacco are still other crops important in Chinese rural economy. Compared with that in most Western countries, the production of these crops is more intensive because of the absence of hay and other fodder crops required for the animal industry of such countries. In this respect China is more like Japan, India, and even Soviet Russia than like the United States or Western Europe.

The growing of two or more crops a year on nearly two thirds of the cultivated land is one way by which the Chinese have adjusted production to the density of population. The trends in kind and proportion of crops grown indicate that crops producing more food and requiring more labor per acre are in the ascendancy, to meet the needs of an increasing population.

Agriculture is more self-sufficient in China than in most Western countries; but still China has a highly developed civilization, and the farmer needs ready money for many purchases, as do farmers of other countries. He must pay for such necessaries as salt and oil, for the occasional meats and other delicacies that enrich his diet on festive occasions, for utensils and wearing apparel, for tobacco or other such luxuries, for schooling and recreation, for weddings and funerals, and for religious observances. Cash for these wants are supplied through the sale of such crops as tobacco, opium, peanuts, rapeseed, cotton, cocoons or raw silk, and, to a lesser extent in proportion to the total crop raised (although the total value may be as great), from soybeans, wheat, green beans, kaoliang, field peas, sweet potatoes, and rice. Often he sells his superior food products such as wheat, and consumes inferior grains such as kaoliang. In order to meet the requirements of both home consumption and ready cash, the Chinese farmer has developed innumerable cropping systems designed to produce the variety of crops required and to utilize his labor more or less throughout the growing season. Some of these systems are suggestive for adoption in other countries having similar climatic, soil, and market conditions. . . .

The kinds of animals raised is still another factor depicting types of land use. Three fourths of the animals in China, in terms of animal units on the basis of food consumed per animal, are used for draft purposes and only one fourth for production purposes—the utilization of the meat, hides, eggs, wool, and the like. The three most important animals are oxen or other cattle for draft purposes, water buffaloes, and hogs. Sheep, mules, donkeys, and goats are other characteristic animals but are of less economic importance. By comparison, in Great Britain only one tenth—and in the United States 22 per cent—of the animals raised are for draft purposes. The density of animal population is, however, surprisingly high in China: 0.34 animal units per crop acre, as compared with 0.70 in Great Britain, 0.23 in the United States, and 0.19 in Japan. China's density of animal population, even in the absence of an animal industry as such, is therefore quite high and means that over a large part of the country the farms are moderately to well-stocked. This is true in spite of the fact that ten per cent of the farms have no animals. This degree of animal density is a large factor in the maintenance of the fertility of the land. In the opinion of three fourths of the farmers, increased use of fertilizer would be profitable, but insufficient capital and unavailable fertilizer curtail such development. Some increase in the animal industry seems possible by using oil cakes and other crop byproducts for feed, and also by a larger use of hill lands for pasture. It would have the advantage of supplying additional fertility, of distributing work more evenly throughout the year, and of providing a more varied and therefore more reliable source of income. At best, however, its development cannot be great, since an acre produces six to seven times as much food-growing crops for direct human consumption as one producing milk, and about 19 times as much food as one producing eggs.

The size of farm is also an indication of the type of land use, since it affects the proportion of land in productive purposes and the efficiency of operation. There are many measures of the size of the farm business other than the number of acres in the farm. The farms of China, which have a median size of 3.31 acres, have a median area of land in crops of 2.37 acres; a crop area of acres harvested, which includes double cropping, of 3.58 acres; a man-equivalent of 2.00 engaged in farm work, or one of 2.5 if all work done on the farm is considered; 1.34 animal units per farm; 0.97 labor animal units; and have a production per farm of 3,492 kilograms of grain, or about one fourteenth of the production in the United States. Of these factors, the man-equivalent is the only one corresponding in amount closely to measures of size in the United States. All the other factors depict a much smaller size of farm business than in the United States or than in most other countries. Farms, when grouped into five size groups, show that very large farms have only 2.5 per cent of the area in farmsteads as compared with 5.8 per cent for small farms. Likewise, small farms have only 89.8 per cent of the land in productive purposes, compared with 93.3 per cent for the very large farms. A denser population, therefore, does not—as one might expect—use a larger proportion of the cultivable land for crop production but, on the contrary, less. Housing and farm administration eat deeply into the small farm acreage where it is most needed. Large farms have the advantage over the small farms also in that parcels and fields are larger and the crop acreage per man-equivalent and per labor animal unit are 2.5 times as great.

The main source of power on Chinese farms is human labor, with animal labor second. This conditions the type of land use. The large amount of available human labor makes it cheap and offers keen competition with other potential sources of power, such as the use of expensive machinery. Hand labor methods continue, therefore, even though the total production might be somewhat less than with the use of machinery.

The dense population and the consequent small size of farm business compel the farmer to utilize every possible opportunity, apart from crop production, to add to his income—whether in the form of objects for direct consumption or in that of articles for sale. No less than one fifth of all the work done on the average Chinese farm is devoted to such subsidiary occupations.

Although labor is plentiful and cheap, still there are periods of peak labor at planting and harvest times when the available labor power is insufficient. This is one of the reasons why women do 13 per cent of all farm work and children seven per cent. The largest proportion, 80 per cent, is performed by men. Peak periods of farm work and large farms make the employment of some hired labor necessary. It represents 15 per cent of all farm work as compared with 30 per cent of all farm work done by hired men in the United States.

Most of the farm labor is for the farm operations of cultivation and harvesting. These operations are also the peak periods of work, and labor-saving devices are imperative. The wheat crop of China is about the size of that in the United States, and it is practically all harvested with sickles within a two-weeks' period in a given section. In the wheat district at harvest time every available human being is out gathering in the harvest—even from the hsien cities (county seats)—for people who do not cut their own wheat, or who are not employed to cut for others, go out and participate in gleaning—an inalienable right through a custom of centuries. Often the harvest fields present the spectacle of more gleaners than legitimate harvesters. In some sections even young girls, who ordinarily must stay indoors, are allowed to come out and assist in the harvest.

The amount of human labor involved in crop production in China is large. The man-equivalent required to grow one acre of wheat is 26 days, compared with 1.2 days in the United States; one acre of cotton in China, 53 days, compared with 14 days in the United States; one acre of corn, 23 days, compared with 2.5 days in the United States. Even the labor animal requirement is higher in China than in the United States, because the animals are often small or weak, implements are crude, and few animals are driven at one time. Wheat requires eight days animal labor in China, compared with 3.4 days in the United States; cotton, eight days, compared with seven days, and corn, five days, compared with 5.7 days. . . .

All these factors characterizing the type of land use portray an intensive type of use compared with that in Western countries. The next consideration is the success obtained in the present type of land use. Success may be measured by a number of factors, such as yields, production per capita, wages of farm labor, taxation of land, the standard of living, and population.

The rather intensive use of land in China, so far as the nature of her crops is concerned, does not, however, show a very intensive culture in terms of yields. The yields of rice are quite high, higher than those of Japan but lower than those of the United States. Wheat yields are similar to those in the United States. In general, China's yields are better than those of India or Russia, not as high as those of Japan, and are less favorable than those of Italy, Germany, Great Britain, and the United States. Floods, droughts, soil erosion, insufficient fertilization, absence of control of insects and diseases, and inferior seeds are among the factors accounting for this situation. Production in terms of grain equivalent of 446 kilograms per capita of farm population is very low. On a basis of production per man-equivalent (one farmer working a full year), China produces only 1,400 kilograms—compared with 20,000 kilograms in the United States, or one fourteenth as much. A farmer who produces little cannot expect to have very much of this world's goods. The dense population in relation to resources is primarily responsible for this situation, and success in the use of land is very greatly dependent upon the number of people on the land. . . .

Moreover, the type of land use in relation to the large farm population does not give full employment. Wages of farm labor, including all perquisites such as food, are only 86 yuan per year. Only a little over one third of the able-bodied men are engaged in full-time work, and over one half are employed only part time. This idle time averages 1.7 months per able-bodied man. It is the winter months which are responsible for four fifths of the idle time. Sickness averages six days per able-bodied man. This unemployment does not prevent labor shortage during peaks of labor, particularly at planting and harvest time. Such shortage was reported by over two thirds of the localities. In other words, the hand methods in use prevent a more equal distribution of labor throughout the year. Labor-saving devices for these peak periods would obliterate this difficulty and would permit some of the farm population to give full time to other pursuits. The development of professions and industry is, in part, dependent upon labor-saving machinery for operations requiring unusual amounts of labor.

Taxation is relatively high, U.S. $1.79 per acre (1929-1932), compared with U.S. $0.46 for all land in farms in the United States in 1932. Even in the better farming districts of the United States, land taxes were only between U.S. $0.90 and U.S. $1.15. The higher taxation does not represent a greater ability of the Chinese farmers to pay, but rather a policy of requiring such payments. This policy, again, is only in part attributable to a national emergency; in part it derives from wasteful methods of tax collection and from an unfortunate situation in many parts of China which places the heaviest burdens on forms of production that permit easy collection at the source and permit other forms of income to escape taxation.

Success in the use of land as revealed in the standard of living can be measured by the amount and quantity of food consumed, the kind of housing, clothing, and furnishing, the amount of debt and savings, and the expenditures for special occasions such as weddings and funerals. Nutrition is an important measure of living standards, since about two thirds of the family budget is expended upon food. Three fourths of this food is produced on the farmer's own farm, nearly one fourth is purchased, and one per cent is collected from wild plants or received as gifts. Products supplied by the farm are grains, seeds of leguminous plants, tuber crops, leafy vegetables, and fruits. Those chiefly purchased are vegetable oils, sugar, and animal products. Wheat is more universally found in the diet than rice, three fourths of the families consuming wheat compared with only one half consuming rice. The amount of food energy consumed varies in sufficiency with the year and the locality. On the average for all localities studied, the amount of food energy was above the minimum requirement of 2,800 calories per adult-male unit per day. Some localities had an overabundance and other localities a serious insufficiency. The sources of this food energy are largely vegetarian, nearly 98 per cent being from plant origin and only 2.3 per cent from animal products. This is in great contrast to the situation in the United States where nearly two fifths of the food energy consumed by farmers comes from animal products. As already explained, it is the consumption of vegetable products rather than animal products which enables the Chinese farmers to eke out a living on such small amounts of land. The nutritive value of this Chinese diet, however, is not wholly satisfactory, not so much because of its being chiefly vegetarian, but because the grains, such as rice and wheat, are too highly milled and because not enough of the leafy vegetables are raised and consumed. This is shown by the low calcium intake, which in turn makes the calcium-phosphorus ratio too low for the effective use of the phosphorus, which would otherwise be adequate; by the source of protein, which while adequate, still is not of the best quality for growth; and by low intakes of vitamin D and probably of vitamins A and C. . . .

Nutrition requirements, therefore, demand some changes in the type of land use to improve its success. Among these changes are a shift in kinds of staple products grown, such as more soybeans in certain localities, the growing of more fruits and vegetables, and possibly some increase in the poultry industry, and the introduction, to a very limited extent, of the dairy industry for milk.

Clothing as a measure of standard of living is largely from one of the cheapest raw materials, cotton—nine tenths of the work garments and three fourths of the dress garments being of this material. It is a satisfactory material for summer wear; but for winter in the colder climates the padded cotton garments are clumsy and apparently not entirely effective in providing the necessary warmth. Wool, although more expensive, affords greater protection in cold climates.

Farm buildings, including residences, vary in size, in materials of construction, and in monetary value. They average over 1,600 cubic feet of space per farm when the height is measured to the eaves. The walls of one half of such buildings are of tamped earth, or earth brick. Burnt brick is used in one fourth of all the buildings. One half of the buildings have tile roofs and one fourth thatch roofs. Over seven eighths of the floors are of earth. The interior and exterior walls are plastered in some sections, and more commonly on the larger than smaller farms. Whitewashing the outside of buildings is common in the Yangtze Delta. Ceilings are rare and the rooms usually extend to the rafters. The value of these buildings is perhaps the best measure of their quality, averaging approximately U.S. $175 per farm, compared with an average value in the United States of U.S. $2,169 in 1930—a ratio even greater than the difference in productive capacity. There may not be, however, quite so great a difference in the net welfare of the individual, although probably nearly so.

There are, on the average, 1.3 rooms per person; but many of these rooms have the combined use of dwelling and housing of equipment, grain, and livestock. Windows are few because of fear of thieves and in many places for superstitious reasons. The houses are poorly ventilated and lighted; floors are often damp and not easily kept clean; the earth walls are insecure in sections subject to flood or heavy rains; and the thatched roofs are fire hazards.

These houses are rather scantily furnished with an average of 28 pieces of all kinds of furniture, such as beds, benches, stools, tables, chests, closets, and sometimes chairs. Nearly four sevenths of such furniture is unpainted, and about one fifth is rough and unplaned.

The amount of debt and savings, in a degree, is a measure of the adequacy of the living standard. Two fifths of the farm families reported debts, averaging 76 yuan per farm, of which only about one fourth was for productive purposes. Only one per cent of the debt was in mortgaged land, a situation far different from that in other countries such as the United States. Some farmers are badly in debt, and usury in some districts is a serious problem. However, the most important source of credit is from relatives and friends, two fifths being so obtained, and this source probably does not represent extortion except in such special cases as with Wang Lung's uncle in *The Good Earth*. Merchants, landlords, and shops supply most of the remainder. These three classes of moneylenders often bleed the farmer to the limit, and for this reason better sources of credit are imperative.

Only one fifth of the farmers reported savings, averaging 192 yuan, though under-reporting probably occurred more for this item than for debts. Savings in the form of money loans amounted to 202 yuan for farmers having the item; in stored agricultural products, 209 yuan; in hoarded money, 139 yuan; and in agricultural products loaned to others, 78 yuan. It is seen, therefore, that while some farmers may be badly in debt, others have substantial savings.

Special expenditures for weddings, funerals, and the like are generally a measure of the farmer's prosperity. These expenditures averaged 152 yuan per family per year. A wedding costs four months' family income and exceeds the yearly income of a hired farm laborer. Funerals cost three months' family income and dowries nearly three months' family income. Such expenditures are, of course, not of annual occurrence.

In terms of standard of living, the success in use of land is not very great. This may be ascribed more to the density of the farm population, 1,500 per square mile of cultivated area, than to type of land use. A birth rate of at least 38 persons per 1,000 persons, and a death rate probably over 27 persons per 1,000 persons for the year studied, indicates a doubling of the population every 65 years. Great calamities have in the past interfered with such a rapid increase over that length of a period. Patriarchal families represent 30 per cent of all families, the remaining 70 per cent being of the ordinary primary type found in most other countries—of husband, wife, and children. These families average 5.21 persons in size. Size of family is in close association with size of farm—showing the effect of a dense population. Small farms have families of only 3.96 persons per farm as compared with 7.31 persons per farm on very large farms. This farm population has only a meager education. Less than 50 per cent of the male and only two per cent of the female population, seven years of age or above, ever attended school. Of those who have received an education, thirty per cent in the case of the males had four years of schooling, and one per cent in that of the females averaged three years. The central fact about marriage is that everyone marries and stays married until the death of either the husband or the wife. More than one half of the males and four fifths of the females married under 20 years of age. As to expectation of life, one half of the population dies before the age of 28 years —a tremendous economic loss even if one considers only the investment in such persons.

5

STATE AND SOCIETY
IN NINETEENTH=CENTURY CHINA

Franz Michael

Communist China has broken with the Chinese cultural tradition, which it attacks and condemns. This break was prepared in
part by the transformation of China during the declining years of
imperial rule and in Republican times. But whereas this period
was marked by the disintegration and disappearance of old institutions and some uncertainty about things to come, a new, rigid
doctrine and social structure are now being introduced to integrate
a new society within a totalitarian state. The old values have been
discarded, but some of the organizational patterns of the past have
been carried over, or have reappeared in the new system. The
Communists are attempting to impose their system on Chinese
society through the agency of an ideologically oriented elite which
not only holds official position in government but also controls
society itself. The degree of success which this system achieves may
depend in part on the extent to which Chinese society has been
prepared by its tradition to accept a centralized bureaucratic state
working through a trained elite. In addition to helping us to assess
the degree of preconditioning in China for Communist rule, an
analytical study of imperial China may provide us with a greater
understanding of the social and political techniques which a
bureaucratic state employs, and which become of such special im-

Dr. Michael, Professor of History, University of Washington, Seattle, is
the author of *The Origin of Manchu Rule in China* (1942) and of
numerous articles on modern Chinese history. This article is based on
data derived from a number of studies undertaken by the author and
colleagues in a cooperative research project on modern Chinese history
at the Far Eastern and Russian Institute, University of Washington. It is
reprinted with permission from *World Politics*, Vol. 7, No. 3 (April 1955),
419-433. Copyright © 1955 by the Princeton University Press.

portance for a totalitarian government. What, then, were the key
features of the imperial state and society which the Communists
have retained or replaced in their own way, and what was the role
played by the educated elite of the past?

The imperial state aimed at a strong control over Chinese
society. The struggle to keep an all-powerful central rule was the
dominant concern of every Chinese dynasty. The center of all
authority was the emperor and the court, the embodiment of the
interests of the state. Serving the emperor was a group of officials,
small in number compared with the size of the country and the
population, and with the importance of the functions to be carried
out. These officials represented the interests of the state as a whole
—its concern with the well-being or acquiescence of all groups of
the population. The last Chinese dynasty had in addition special
support from a group which served the state without being a part
of Chinese society. The Manchus had come as conquerors from the
frontier of the Chinese empire, with their forces militarily organized
into units known as "banners." When the Manchu dynasty was set
up, the Manchu banners were kept apart from the Chinese people
and the bannermen remained an inner core of dynastic supporters
used both as a military force and in key official positions. But these
bannermen were only a small group, largely unqualified for the
complex tasks of Chinese administration, and thus the Manchu
dynasty, like its predecessors, had to recruit its state administration
from Chinese society. To fill the positions in the state administration, the emperor had to be able to draw on a social stratum that
was willing and equipped to fill the ranks of bureaucracy and to
carry out public functions. This social stratum was the scholar-
gentry, a group of educated men whose training gave them a monopoly claim on the holding of office within the imperial bureaucracy.

The bureaucratic aspect of the Chinese imperial state has been
recognized, although its importance has sometimes been under-
estimated. What has not been recognized, however, is the role
played by the members of the scholar-gentry, beyond their part as
state officials, in the carrying out of public functions in society. The
Manchu dynasty, like its predecessors, set up the comparatively
small number of not more than 40,000 official positions for the
management of the most urgent tasks in central and local government. At the lowest level of the official hierarchy was the district
magistrate, who with his limited personal staff had to administer an
area with an average population of 200,000. Many of the public

functions in the districts and even in the provinces could not possibly be handled by these officials, or by them alone. Hence, to the much larger group of the scholar-gentry fell the task of managing most of the public functions in the administrative areas where they resided. Not only the imperial state but the society itself was bureaucratic—that is, managed by institutionalized public functionaries set apart from the mass of the population. Like the members of the modern totalitarian parties, the members of the scholar-gentry formed a link between society and state, fulfilling their functions in both.

But here the similarity ends. The Chinese imperial state was not totalitarian. Although in theory the emperor was omnipotent, he had no control over the Chinese ideological and social system, even though he tried to influence it. Imperial China did not know the terror of totalitarianism with its organized penetration into all spheres of life. For this reason, the problem of central control over the official organization and, most of all, over the scholar-gentry was never completely solved and remained a constant concern of the dynastic government. The scholar-gentry's interest in the process of state administration could be superseded by their concern to maintain the framework of society and to protect the interests of their group and of their locality, once the state administration became disorderly and lost control. This potential conflict of loyalties and interests, leading again and again to the downfall of dynastic governments, created a continued tension which constituted the dynamics of Chinese bureaucratic development.

Our analysis of the Chinese state and society derived from the last century of imperial rule will thus be focused on this decisive social group, the scholar-gentry. There was a deep social and legal gulf between the small group of so-called *shen-shih,* the educated, the literati, or, as we call them, the gentry, and the large mass of commoners—the poor peasants in the thousands of villages, and the more well-to-do artisans and merchants in the towns. The commoners looked to the gentry for leadership, and whether in appreciation of the merits of their many services, or in fear and bitterness because of their oppression, they respected them as men of learning, as their superiors.

During the last centuries of imperial China, the gentry was a clearly recognizable group. Its members were holders of academic degrees. These degrees, gained in official examinations, or in some cases acquired through purchase, gave the holders their privileged

position in society. And only on the basis of such an academic
degree could anyone receive a government position. The gentry
were thus a certified educated group.

Around 1,100,000 persons at the beginning of the nineteenth
century and 1,500,000 by the end of the century belonged to this
privileged group. The gentry, together with their families, who
shared their privileged position, comprised about 5,500,000 to 7,500,-
000 people, or roughly from 1½ to 2 per cent of the population.
Only a very small minority of the gentry could fill the 40,000 official
positions which the dynastic government had established. This
meant that even with a comparatively high turnover, the large
majority of the gentry never came to hold public office. Important
as it was, the monopoly on public office was therefore only one of
the major aspects of the gentry's role in China. Those who never
held office or who were temporarily out of office were, however, by
no means excluded from public affairs. On their own, or in cooperation with the officials, they dealt with the many interests of their
communities for which official government had no time.

Manifold were the functions thus carried on by the gentry in
settling issues through local arbitration, in sponsoring and organizing local charity and welfare matters, grain storage, rice kitchens,
and the like, and, most of all, in public works: the vital field of
flood prevention, irrigation, and canalization. The building of
dams, dikes, canals, roads, and bridges was planned, organized, and
supervised by the gentry. In these functions, and especially in the
field of public works, gentry activity often went beyond the
boundaries of a single district and concerned joint works for larger
areas in the province. And it must be emphasized that these public
functions of the gentry were carried out not within the confines of
privately held property, but within the political borders of the
district and province to which the gentry belonged. Often such
activity required the approval of officials. Sometimes it led to joint
official-gentry direction and financing, or an officially initiated
program was carried out under the guidance and control of local
gentry. Indeed, there probably were few public works programs in
which the gentry had not some share of responsibility. In this vital
field of public affairs and economic control, the gentry thus played
a very important part. In times of crisis, as will be shown, this part
grew in importance and was extended to military organization and
activities as well, which in turn required financial control of
regular tax sources.

If we turn from the sphere of practical affairs to the still more important areas of culture and moral beliefs, the gentry's central role is manifest. Confucianism was accepted by the state as the official ideology, but it was studied, taught, believed in, and preached by the gentry, who gave it reality as the focal force of Chinese culture. The gentry were educated and examined in the tenets of Confucianism; and they were understood to have mastered its moral principles as a result of their education. This is not the place to describe the value system of Confucian beliefs, with its emphasis on the dignity of human relations and the importance of social responsibility, represented and interpreted in so many different forms throughout imperial history. In the nineteenth century, Confucianism was still a strong moral force. Then, as before, the gentry were regarded as the guardians of the Confucian tradition. In the eyes of Chinese society, they were the educated elite of morally superior men, qualified to lead society. They preserved and carried on the Chinese cultural tradition. They were the writers, the philosophers, the painters, the poets, and the men of affairs who together made up the greatness of Chinese civilization.

Apart from the literary tradition carried on by the gentry, their cultural activities had a practical side. Teaching was for many a profession. The upkeep of temples or memorial arches, participation in local sacrifices and in the so-called village lectures (*hsiang yüeh*), in which themes from the doctrine were extolled, were important gentry functions. And in their daily life and practices, as well as in the higher field of scholarship, the gentry gave Chinese society its ideological character.

These social functions of the gentry cannot be sharply distinguished from the official functions of the government. They were often intertwined. Whether in or out of office, whether in the interest of the state or of the home community or area, it was one and the same social group that managed public affairs. But the large majority of the gentry were without official position and carried out their activities as social functions, without which, it is true, the government could not have operated. The gentry's dominant position was therefore based not on its monopoly of office-holding alone, but on the whole part it played in Chinese society.

This part was indicated also by the gentry's recognized status and privileged position. The gentry had a preferred position before the law, with a special procedure for the prosecution of gentry crimes and exemptions from humiliating punishment; they had privileges giving them social prestige, such as appearance in public with runners or outriders, with special gowns and hats and buttons; most of all, they had economic privileges. In recognition of their gentry services, they were free from the *corvée,* and they could use their position to escape the onerous surtaxes and lighten their general tax burden. Altogether, the gentry were apart from and above the mass of the commoners, on a par with the officials before whom the commoners had to prostrate themselves; the officials, themselves members of the gentry, were equals with whom social contact made easy the promotion of common interests.

This elevated position of the gentry in Chinese society was therefore based on their accepted role as managers of public affairs. The gentry themselves believed in such a responsibility. The statement of their obligation by Fan Chung-yen in Sung times: "Hsien t'ien-hsia chih yu erh yu; hou t'ien-hsia chih lo erh lo," "To be first in worrying about the world's troubles and last in the enjoyment of its pleasures," indicates their feeling of dedication to selfless service which, if not always lived up to, was believed in as a standard of gentry behavior. And in the mid-nineteenth century the famous scholar, Tseng Kuo-fan, called the gentry to battle in defense of their society. When the Taipings threatened Confucianism with their new ideology. Tseng exclaimed:

> How could that be a change that only concerns our Ch'ing dynasty? No, it is a serious change that concerns our entire civilization (*ming chiao*) from its very beginnings, and makes our Confucius and our Mencius cry with grief at the nine wells. How can anyone who can read and write remain quietly seated, hands in sleeves, without thinking of doing something about it?

To arouse the gentry to organize their communities and to lead them in the fight, he used again and again the famous quotation from Ku Yen-wu at the end of the Ming dynasty: "T'ien-hsia hsing wang, p'i-fu yu tse," "The fortune or misfortune of the world rests on the shoulders of each of us." Leadership of the community, more urgent in times of emergency, was always an accepted task for the gentry. The gentry's knowledge of the principles of human affairs and human relations and of the ethical tenets which were believed to rule them qualified the gentry to organize and lead the people in these public tasks. The basis of the gentry's power was knowledge and the acceptance of their intellectual status by society.

This definition runs counter to a frequently held opinion that the position and power of the Chinese gentry were based on land-ownership. The ownership of land, from which the gentry are believed by some to have derived their main income, is held to determine, in an agricultural society such as China, the gentry's local power and with it their dominant role in society and state. What was the gentry's position in Chinese economy? Their public functions included, as we have seen, the management and control of public works as well as official administrative control of the economy, and this was reflected in their income. A study of the nineteenth-century Chinese national product and of the gentry's share in it, based on figures of the 1880's, has provided us with economic data that parallel our findings on the importance of the gentry's public role in managing Chinese society and state. As the dominant group in society, monopolizing government office, the gentry could be expected to have had a share of the national income larger than the group's proportional size in the total population. Our figures indicate that the gentry—making up about two per cent of the population—received about 23 per cent of the national income. Of greater importance, however, is a breakdown of this gentry income according to the sources from which it was derived. Much of the irregular income from official positions or public functions—the bribes, the squeeze, and all the other extras that were improper and therefore secret—is not easy to ascertain or to determine in figures. It is therefore calculated very conservatively in this study, and it is possible that this sort of income was considerably higher. The regular income is more easily evaluated. On the basis of this regular income and a conservative estimate of the irregular income, the total gentry income is estimated as being derived almost 50 per cent from services, including official salaries, compensations for gentry service of many kinds, such activities as teaching, and so forth; a little less than a third came from landownership; and about one fifth from entrepreneurial or business activities of one kind or another, the latter figure increasing slightly toward the end of the nineteenth century. This, it must be understood, was the proportionate income for the gentry as a whole.

These figures become even more remarkable when divided among the various groups within the gentry itself. We believe that a distinction can be made between the upper gentry, consisting of the holders of the higher examination degrees and official ranks, on the one hand, and the rank and file of the lower degree-holders, whether they were possessors of examination or purchased degrees, on the other. The former group, the upper gentry, consisted in our estimate of about 14 per cent of the total gentry, leaving the large majority of 86 per cent as lower gentry. One would expect to find the income from rents going largely to the lower gentry, which excluded all officeholders and the most influential gentry figures. But the data indicate that most of the rent income, about three fourths of it, went to the upper gentry. In fact, it went to a very small proportion of them. Less than ten per cent of the upper gentry had the largest share of the total rent income of the gentry. These figures show us that the large majority of the gentry, especially the lower gentry, but also most of the upper gentry, received their main income not from land but from public services. The vast majority of the gentry thus received their main income from their paramount public functions. And those upper gentry families who were large landowners, and of whom we know (for instance, Tseng Kuo-fan's family), usually acquired their land after they gained prominence and wealth in public service. With the division of property through inheritance laws and the uncertainty of positions of political influence, the acquisition of landed property was not the basis of political power.

We believe these findings support our view of the character of Chinese society, a society in which an educated elite, as officials of the state and as the leading social group, managed vital public functions—including the all-important public works—and derived its dominant position from this monopoly of management.

Any state organization that depends, as did the Chinese state, on the services of such a monopoly group faces a tremendous problem of integration and of central control. The state had to curb and restrain the individual, clique, and group interests of the members of the gentry, and to merge them with the common interests of the whole community. This interest of the Chinese state was most obviously expressed by the emperor and the dynastic family itself. To get control of the gentry, to get them into his "basket," to have them depend on his central authority rather than on an autonomous authority of their own, was a main aim of the emperor's government. And the imperial Chinese state had developed an elaborate, intricate, and highly sophisticated system to gain and maintain such central control.

The control of the gentry was, of course, only one part of the broader problem of dynastic authority in a society the framework of which the emperors could use but could not determine. Within that society, other organizational rivals challenged at times the power of the official government. From the time of the Sung dynasty at least, secret societies and their branches had formed illegal organizations within the state and created periodic open rebellions against the authority of the existing government. These groups had a different type of social leadership and often in their original form maintained a more equalitarian ideology derived from Buddhist or Taoist beliefs. But for any larger positive effort to create administrations of their own, secret societies or other such groups depended on the services of qualified educated men. In any political conflict, there was thus always the struggle to maintain a central authority over the obedience and services of the educated elite, and to limit and curb the possibility of its forming or supporting rival organizations.

The measures of control used under the Ch'ing dynasty were in the main not new, but were in several ways more refined than those of its dynastic predecessors. The examination system itself was an important measure of control. Through it, the state determined who became a member of the gentry and through what qualifications. The quotas which were set for the examinations limited the size of the gentry and kept it manageable. Regardless of the vast number of local applicants, the quotas provided only a limited number of gentry members for each district to carry out the gentry functions. The government's control over the content of the examinations permitted it to stress the official aspects of Confucian philosophy or the importance of form. Review examinations, control of the gentry through the local schools, and stipends supervised by state-appointed educational commissioners were other checks. Indeed, the constantly induced preoccupation of the gentry with preparation for examinations—"the examination life"—was a method of channeling the gentry's energies that permitted little time for undesirable developments in thought or action.

These measures, which can only be touched upon here, dealt with the gentry itself. Others dealt with the communities. Main examples were the *pao-chia* and *li-chia* systems, which, according to the original plan, handled local police control and tax collection, respectively. By dividing the communities arbitrarily into such subadministrative units and placing commoners in the position of local agents of the state, responsible to the officials for security or tax payment, the government undermined the autonomous position of the communities and handicapped their leadership. Although such measures did not function as planned for any great length of time, they had a stimying effect on the communities, providing at least a temporary safeguard against any form of local autonomy. While the state used the gentry for local control, it thus introduced at the same time its own direct local organizations.

More sophisticated still were the measures, in force up until the Taiping Rebellion, to maintain central control within the group of gentry serving the state as officials. No official was to serve in his home district or province, so that there would be no chance for the growth of local roots of power. For the same reason, officials held office for only short periods of time and were frequently shifted from place to place. Another precaution taken at the expense of effective administration was both the division and the overlapping of the functions of officials on all top and intermediate levels. An intricate system of divided authorities, of mutual checks and secret reports, was designed to keep all threads in the hands of the emperor. To manage it, however, he needed an inner core of officials of special loyalty. Studies on official careers indicate that there was an inner group of central officials into which those who had once gained important positions in the provinces were not again admitted. This central group was then expected to represent, like the emperor himself, the interests of the central government with which it was so closely linked.

In addition, the Manchu dynasty used its own people as a check on Chinese society. The Manchus, artificially kept apart from the Chinese in their banner organizations, were used as garrisons in strategic locations as a military safeguard for the dynasty. Moreover, they held jointly with Chinese the key offices of the central government and filled some of the key positions in the provinces.

This whole elaborate mechanism for maintaining central authority succeeded only temporarily. Toward the end of each dynastic period, the very problems which it tried to exclude recurred. In the nineteenth century, the Ch'ing government was in decline. The growing economic strength and independence of the local gentry, the growing corruption and demoralization of the administration, paralyzed by its own system of controls, brought a weakening of the central authority and a strengthening of local and eventually regional autonomy, in which both local officials and scholar-gentry became increasingly independent of the central government. The less effective the government became, the more opportunities there were for local mismanagement and exploitation, and the more local unrest, banditry, and uprisings resulted. The impotence of the official administration gave local leaders, secret society heads, or local bullies the opportunity to expand their influence. And the gentry's social functions, which had fitted so well into the state system, took on a different character when the administration and its central control crumbled. First things came first, and the gentry, too, organized communities for defense in the spreading local struggle. Quarrels between local communities or clans, resistance against exploitation, and defense against the growing danger of banditry, itself caused by economic misery, led to the development of local military organizations. The regular government troops became corrupt and ineffective, together with the rest of the administration, and local forces took matters into their own hands. The very danger appeared which the government had tried to avoid, the emergence of local leaders with their own resources of power. The gentry or secret society leaders who formed local corps commanded forces personally loyal to them. They controlled areas from which they derived their financial support, and they built up staff organizations of men appointed by them and loyal to their group. As soon as these organizations grew beyond the level of local intercommunity rivalry and affected a larger region, they became an open political challenge to the dynastic regime.

The Taiping Rebellion, in the middle of the nineteenth century, thus grew from the level of local organization and local conflicts into a rebellious movement, through the appeal of a fanatical ideology taken in part from Christianity, with precepts that seemed to promise correction of some of the political, social, and economic ills of the time. The dynastic government was truly incapable of defense. But the local gentry, who could not cooperate with a movement so alien to the cultural tradition which they represented, set up their own defenses based on their own local sources of power. When the official leadership through the state failed, the gentry expanded their activities. They formed military organizations, and to finance them they at first levied contributions but soon established their own tax organizations, which were practically uncontrolled by the state. From local beginnings grew regional machines, with military, financial, and administrative power.

The story of the buildup of regional armies out of gentry-led local corps by Tseng Kuo-fan and others like him cannot be told here. After trying to keep down these regional defenders of the Chinese cultural tradition, the dynastic government, following the defeat of its own armies, finally had no choice but to grant to these men the actual administrative offices of the provinces. These new regional leaders and their military organizations were far more successful in building up administrative and military control over the areas within their reach than were the Taipings themselves. Area by area, and city by city, they destroyed the Taiping forces until they took the Taiping capital, Nanking, and crushed the rebellion.

But while fighting for the government of the Ch'ing dynasty, these gentry leaders established their own power. Even after the crisis was over, some of them retained their military forces, their financial resources, and the administrative organizations which they had created in the areas occupied by them. The dynastic government had no choice but to continue to appoint these men to positions as governors and governors-general in these areas, and thus to sanction the growth of regional power. Even if individual leaders were removed, the organizations remained, and while the government retained the authority to appoint officials, to dismiss them, or to shift them from place to place, it could not destroy the organizational roots of their power or the personal loyalties of officers and officials who had been the protégés of such leaders. When the head of such an organization was removed to another province, he took with him some of his troops, offered appointments to his friends, and frequently established new sources of income without giving up his old ones. The elaborate system of separation of gentry from officials, of mutual checks on the officials, and of division of functions and authority broke down. There developed a new type of provincial governor-general, who had military, financial, and administrative power of his own and had to be consulted by the throne on major policy matters. With the growing importance of foreign relations, some of these men even began to deal directly with foreign powers. Chinese foreign policy, then, became linked with the inner struggle.

Why did this system of regional developments not lead to a new reintegration of power? To attempt an answer would carry us far beyond the scope of this article. But it may be pointed out that the leading group in society and state, the scholar-gentry, lost its functional as well as its intellectual and spiritual basis at the turn of the century, partly as the result of the influence of the West.

The leaders of the first regional army formed against the Taiping Rebellion were, like their commander Tseng Kuo-fan, Confucian scholars who aimed at maintaining the traditional gentry ideals. When the movement of regional organization spread from the rural interior to the coast and the coastal cities, the traditional social basis and, with it, its moral force were lost. The regional organization of Li Hung-chang exploited the new commercial and industrial opportunities on the coast and applied to them the methods of gentry-official control formerly exercised in agricultural China. A last attempt to revive the Confucian state on the basis of a reformed Confucian belief was made by the philosopher K'ang Yu-wei, but it failed. And with the end of the traditional educational system, marked by the abolition of examinations, the sustaining moral force of the dominant scholar-gentry class disappeared, and so did the traditional scholar-gentry itself. There survived into Republican times a residue of bureaucratic tradition which has reappeared in the new Communist bureaucratic state and society, where a new indoctrinated elite plays a leading part, but without any of the ethical values once held high by the Confucian scholars.

From this analysis, many parallels suggest themselves between the institutions of the imperial state and society and the role of the gentry, on the one hand, and the institutions of the Communist state and the Communist Party, on the other. The general management of affairs by an elite group; the relationship of functions handled by members of the elite through their official positions to those handled through their role in society; the role of the elite as carrier and propagator of the dominant ideology; the restricted size of the elite group and the control of admission to it; the channeling of thought—in all these and in many other characteristics, the imperial structure shows strong similarities to the Communist system. What is different today is that the leadership of the elite party is at the same time at the head of the state government. What is also different is the Communist combination of a central institutional control with a control over the ideology itself. No independent value system remains, and the ideological independence of the gentry which made possible the inner balance of the imperial system has been replaced by an ideological centralism in which right and wrong are always determined by the total authority of those on the Communist throne.

6

THE KUOMINTANG: ITS DOCTRINE, ORGANIZATION, AND LEADERSHIP

Ch'ien Tuan=sheng

It is certain that before 1919 or 1920 Sun Yat-sen was a combination of a revolutionary and Western democrat. As a revolutionary he was impatient; he could not tolerate any regime which seemed to him to be bad. As a democrat, he wanted to see China become a democracy. It was the interplay of his revolutionary temperament and his democratic inclinations that sometimes made for a conflict within his personality. To understand him, one must keep both in mind. One must not, because of his emphasis on party tutelage which is indistinguishable from party dictatorship, deny to Sun Yat-sen genuine democratic inclinations. Sun Yat-sen understood democracy and up to 1919 never lost sight of it.

But beginning from 1919 the revolutionary aspect of his personality dominated his whole being, more than ever before. He was more eager than ever to wipe out the old regime and to install his party in power. He gladly embraced whoever and whatever could be of service to him in this regard. With some reluctance he deviated from his old stand. But deviate he did. One need only scan the differences between the Manifesto of the party issued on January 1, 1923, and that of its First Congress a year later to see his reluctance and also his shifting of ground.

Dr. Ch'ien, one of the foremost political scientists in modern China, wrote the book from which this selection is reprinted while at Harvard University after World War II. Since his return to Mainland China, he has been very much in eclipse. Reprinted with permission, with deletions, from Chapter 8 of *The Government and Politics of China* (Cambridge: Harvard University Press, 1950). Copyright 1950 by the President and Fellows of Harvard College.

SUN YAT-SEN'S REORGANIZED IDEAS

Of the circumstances which led to the reorganization of the Kuomintang in 1924, some account has been given in a previous chapter. The principal influence in that reorganization came from Moscow. But the Soviet influence could not have brought itself to bear upon Sun Yat-sen had it not been synchronized with the rise of the student movement which was antagonistic to the imperialism of the Powers and the traditionalism of the Chinese state at one and the same time. . . .

Sun Yat-sen's principal aim was to give a new vitality to his party in order that his revolution might soon succeed. He understood why the Russian Communist Party had succeeded, and he admired the organization and techniques of that party. If his own party could come to possess the energies and capacities of the Russian party, all else was of secondary importance. He did not like communism, and still less the dialectics of Marxism. But he was not worried by the inroad of such things in his party. He needed an ally to advise him on the improvement of party organization and tactics. He was eager to furnish himself with a strong and reliable military backing, a thing sorely needed for the establishment of a base. On this, he also needed Russian advice. To achieve his over-all purpose, in short, he needed Soviet aid. In order to get that aid, he was naturally willing to be allied with the Soviet, and if his allies should insist on his collaborating with the Chinese Communists and on his enlisting the support of labor and the peasantry as conditions of aid, he would not mind. That is why the so-called Three Policies, "Russian Alliance," "Admission of the Communists," and "Emphasis on the Agrarian and Labor Policy," though not formally enunciated by either the First or Second Party Congresses, were clearly discernible in the spirit of the Manifesto of the First Congress, dated January 30, 1924.

On the other hand, the Three People's Principles as stated in this Manifesto had undergone great changes as the result of Sun Yat-sen's new orientation. If one sets the year 1921 as the line of demarcation and compares the Party's and his own enunciations before and after, one cannot fail to be impressed by the new elements in both the content and the spirit of the Three Principles. In the Kuomintang Manifesto of January 1, 1923, a new chord had already been struck. By the early months of 1924, as evidenced both by the Manifesto of the First Congress and by Sun Yat-sen's lectures on *San Min Chu I*, the change was complete.

Sun Yat-sen's Three Principles of the People are the Principles of *Min-tsu*, *Min-ch'üan*, and *Min-sheng*, or, respectively, People's Nationhood, People's Power, and People's Livelihood. The first two can certainly be rendered as "Nationalism" and "Democracy," for they are not different from them. The Principle of the People's Livelihood is neither socialism nor communism, and to translate it as "Socialism" would be out of place. It is better to let either *Min-sheng* or People's Livelihood stand.

1. *Nationalism*. The nationalist concept of Sun Yat-sen went through three successive phases. The first phase was simple. The Manchus who had ruled over China were considered an alien race denying self-government to the Chinese. Chinese nationalism demanded the liquidation of that group. When the Manchus were gone, the Chinese Republic of 1912 was regarded as a political community in which the five races, the Chinese, the Manchus, the Mongols, the Mohammedans, and the Tibetans, formed one inseparable unit. Nobody cared to subject that vague and confused conception to historical and ethnological analysis. Sun Yat-sen himself was no exception. For years he said almost nothing about his first Principle. In the 1914 statute of his newly christened Chinese Revolutionary Party, it was formally provided that the aims of the party were to fulfill the Principles of People's Power and People's Livelihood. At that time Sun Yat-sen must have felt that his first Principle had been fully realized.

A new interpretation of nationalism began with Sun Yat-sen's own disillusionment with the Powers and with the rise of the student movement and his contact with Soviet ideas. By 1924 the Principle had acquired new meaning and new substance. Nationalism is anti-imperialistic in its external aspect, and embraces self-determination of the racial minorities within the borders of China. It can be realized only by a nationalist revolution against imperialist control and also against the Chinese elements which have conspired with or tolerated the imperialists. Further, the Chinese were also to help other oppressed nations, especially those in the East, to shake off their foreign yokes. It is therefore also to be a world revolution of the oppressed nations. In this, Sun Yat-sen's nationalism differed little, if any, from the Soviet tenets at the time. But in two aspects Sun Yat-sen was uniquely Chinese. First, he was in favor of self-determination for the minorities in China, or, in the words of the Manifesto, the "several nationalities" of China were to enjoy the rights of self-determination and finally to federate themselves into a Chinese republic. Yet at the same time he also said that national assimilation does not run counter to the Principle of Nationalism. Here he seemed to be saying that if the Chinese had succeeded in assimilating other races, the latter need not seek self-determination. Second, Sun Yat-sen continued to cherish the Confucianist idea of a "Great Commonwealth" which would comprise all mankind and would naturally obliterate all national and racial demarcations.

2. *Democracy.* Sun Yat-sen's second Principle also experienced historical changes and graftings. With one exception, there was nothing to show that Sun Yat-sen's earlier concept of the Principle was anything other than the kind of democracy which prevailed in the contemporary West. The exception was that Sun Yat-sen did from very early times advocate a period of tutelage. His party was to enjoy exclusive political power during the period, and the veteran members were even to enjoy political privileges during their lifetime. But this was not to be a thing of permanence; it did not really cut into the principle of democracy.

With the coming of the Soviet antiparliamentarian doctrine, coupled with the revulsion which the failures of the Chinese Parliament had created in him, he began to be harshly critical of the representative democracies of the West, considering them to be both antinationalist and anti-Min-sheng: antinationalist because the Western democracies allowed only self-rule for the dominant race, leaving other nations or races subjected and oppressed; anti-Min-sheng because the capitalists of the Western democracies denied livelihood to the less fortunate classes.

According to Sun Yat-sen, therefore, a tenable Principle of People's Power, or real democracy, must be in full conformity with the other two Principles. He proposed that the people should exercise directly the four powers of election, recall, initiative, and referendum. With these four powers directly exercised by the people, there would be no danger of the people ever losing their power over government. Then he went on to put what he terms "powers and functions" in juxtaposition. While the people should have the full enjoyment of powers, the functions should nevertheless be vested in the unfettered hands of the government equally fully. There were to be five functions—namely, executive, legislative, judicial, control, and examination. With gusto he argued for the separation of the functions of control and examination from the three older powers defined by Montesquieu.

Thus Sun Yat-sen advocated a government capable of the full exercise of five functions or, as he calls it, "an all-function government." At the same time he cast aspersions on the idea of natural rights. In subsequent years this has given rise to a school of interpretation which has done yeoman service to justify the disregard, if not suppression, of popular freedoms, and the emergence of an irresponsible and dictatorial, if not also totalitarian, government. A more sensible interpretation of Sun Yat-sen's second Principle would have emphasized the more positive aspect of his concept of the People's Political Powers, rather than either his criticism of representative democracy or his partisanship for a strong government. In the whole scheme of his second Principle, strong government certainly occupies only an auxiliary place, whereas the enjoyment of full political powers by the people was his main concern.

3. *Min-sheng.* The Livelihood Principle is not so susceptible to fair and intelligent interpretation. That Principle presents both a theory and a number of proposals. Sun Yat-sen was opposed to Karl Marx's materialist interpretation of history. He had no sympathy for the class struggle of Marx. Nor did he accept the Marxian theory of surplus value. He did not quite say that he would oppose his own interpretation of history to the materialism of Marx, but if any of his followers should, as some now do, pit Min-sheng-ism against materialism, or the Min-sheng interpretation of history against the materialist interpretation of history, they certainly cannot be accused of fabrication. Indeed, in his acceptance of an obscure American author's "social interpretation of history" Sun Yat-sen accepted the idea that "livelihood is the central force in social progress, and that social progress is the central force in history; hence the struggle for a living and not material forces determines history." Thinking along this social line, Sun Yat-sen, though recognizing the existence of classes, also repudiated class struggle, and favored conciliation among classes.

As for more concrete proposals, Sun Yat-sen advocated the equalization of land tenure, and the regulation of capital. To achieve the former, he proposed that the unearned increment of land value should accrue to the state. To achieve the latter, he proposed state ownership of principal industries and enterprises. While lack of precision characterizes the latter proposal, a lack of comprehensiveness marks the former. Finally his famous answer to the question, "What is the Principle of Livelihood?"—"It is communism and it is socialism," confounds his readers still further.

In justice to Sun Yat-sen it must be said that his economic thinking was progressive and that he was genuinely interested in the welfare of the little man. But he never formulated a well-thought-out economic theory or a well-planned economic program.

It is then not unfair to observe that the chief innovation in the revised Three Principles of 1924 was the harnessing of anti-imperialist sentiment, which was then popular with the more forward-looking elements of the country, to give the party a new battle cry and to accelerate the downfall of its enemies. The other aspects of the Principles were of no urgent import at the moment and they were still vague and obscure.

IDEOLOGICAL STERILITY AFTER SUN'S DEATH

Thus, the principal objective of the Kuomintang Reorganization of 1923-1924 was to equip the party with a new vigor, with effective revolutionary techniques of organization and agitation, and with a strong and reliable military support behind the whole movement. Such changes as there were in the interpretation of the Three Principles were only incidental to that objective. Accordingly, the significance of the split with the communists in 1927 and then of the break with the Soviet Union depends on the question to what extent these ruptures tended to undermine the vigor of the Kuomintang, both in its use of revolutionary techniques, and in the military support behind them. On the surface, the fact that the Northern Expedition succeeded and the whole country was brought under the Kuomintang seemed to prove that there was no deterioration. One thing was certainly sure, that the Kuomintang lost little of the technique of organization and agitation which they had acquired in the days of collaboration.

But the purge of the communists, not to mention the murder of large numbers of the educated youth who formed such a small fraction of the total Chinese population, certainly also purged the Kuomintang of a group of more militant workers. The exit of the militant elements from the party tended to encourage the incoming of the more conservative and even reactionary elements of Chinese society. Though the revolutionary vigor persisted for a short while after the split, it could not be maintained for long. The Kuomintang became after 1929 not only conservative but also complacent. It was not until 1945, when it was brought face to face with the vigorous program of social and economic reforms of the militant communists, that the Kuomintang again bestirred itself to adopt an equally radical program, at the Sixth Congress in May of that year. But it then found itself lacking in men of vigor and ambition to carry through such a program. In this sense, it is plain that the party was adversely affected by the split with the communists in 1927.

If the split with an outside party adversely affected its vigor, the schisms within prevented the Kuomintang from evolving carefully and logically a body of doctrines which could fit the conditions of China and, at the same time, implement the Three Principles of its founder. One may be for or against deifying a political leader and making his writings sacrosanct, but if deification is to take place one must interpret the writings of the deified in such a way as to give them a consistency and a living quality and yet at the same time not do violence to the original text. Unfortunately, the schisms and later the segmentation which have afflicted the party have also precluded the presentation of sharply distinguished interpretations of Sun Yat-sen's writings, but produced only second-rate and commonplace textual glossaries. The more radical theoreticians were sensitive to accusations of communist leanings; the more conservative were apprehensive of being called reactionaries. All were afraid of being criticized and condemned as unfaithful to the teachings of Sun Yat-sen. The total effect was that few cared or dared to venture beyond textual interpretations.

It is conceivable that if there had been neither schisms nor segmentation and the party had been more united, a different kind of interpretation might have resulted and a democratic political edifice and a program of expansive and egalitarian economic reforms might have been developed from his Second and Third Principles respectively. As it was, the Three Principles remained vague, incoherent, and at points inconsistent with each other and with the actualities, in spite of Sun Yat-sen's nobleness of heart, devotion to the national welfare, and, in general, enlightenment in regard to the future of the country. In this sense the evil effect of the schisms and the segmentation within the party has been profound. . . .

CONGRESSES AND EXECUTIVE COMMITTEES

Like the Russian Communist Party, the structure of the Kuomintang forms a pyramid. In conformity with China's geographical divisions of governmental structure, the Kuomintang has, from the lowest to the highest, four tiers of authority. At the bottom there is the *Ch'ü* Organization; above, corresponding with the *hsien,* there stands the *Hsien* Organization; higher still is the Provincial Organization; at the top of the pyramid stands the Central Organization. Each level of organization maintains an executive and a supervisory committee, elected in the case of the *ch'ü* by party members directly, but in the higher levels by congresses of party delegates, elected in turn by the congresses on a lower level. To illustrate: The party congress of a certain province elects the provincial executive committee and supervisory committee which constitute the provincial organization; the delegates to that provincial congress are in turn elected by the *hsien* congresses of the province.

The *Ch'ü* Organization is the lowest functioning unit. There are, however, below it the *ch'ü* branches. The members of each are supposed to meet often and to discuss matters of interest to the party and perform duties pertaining to them as the élite of the general population.

Then there are some special organizations somewhat distorting the rigorous lines of the pyramid. Members who have no fixed residence, principally the railway employees and the seamen, form themselves into special organizations which are placed under the direct control of the Central Organization. The organization of the Kuomintang members overseas is also irregular and held close to the central body. But the most extraordinary is the party organization in the armed forces—the army, naval, and air units all have their own party organizations. They form a separate pyramid, and are placed directly in the Central Organization.

According to the Statute of the Party, the National Congress, and, after its adjournment, the Central Executive Committee, is the highest organ of party power. The Central Supervisory Committee has only the power of discipline and financial control. All this was modeled after the Russian Communist Party as the latter stood in 1924.

In theory and also in appearance, the Congress has always remained supreme. Whether the Central Executive Committee can still be considered the highest organ depends on its position vis-à-vis the Party Leader, a post which has existed since 1938 and which will be discussed presently. But, in reality, both the Congress and the Central Executive Committee have long become ratification conventions or sounding boards. Neither enjoys the reality of power.

The Congress has always been a large-sized body. In the First Congress there were 150 delegates, and by the Sixth Congress, held in 1945, the number had grown to about 600. If the delegates are elected, the election is usually controlled by the party machine. If they are appointed, as has often been the case, they are under its absolute control. In either case, they cannot be expected either to want or be able to oppose the high leadership of the party. They may talk and at times even voice their grievances, but in the end they always accept what is handed to them.

The size of the Central Executive Committee has also grown rapidly. It grew from one of 24, with 17 reserve members, elected by the First Congress in 1924, to one of 222, with 90 reserve members, elected by the Sixth Congress in 1945. The last elected Central Executive Committee, which is still functioning, is almost as unwieldy as the Congress itself, for, whenever it meets, the Central Supervisory Committee of 104, with 44 reserve members, is also in attendance and in full participation, as is customary with such meetings of the party.

Furthermore, the statutory requirement that the Party Congress should be convened once every two years (originally every year) and the Central Executive Committee every half year, has never been faithfully met. In the course of twenty-four years since the Reorganization of the Party, there have been only six Congresses. The plenary sessions of the Central Executive Committee are more numerous, but they too are held at very irregular intervals. The convening of the Congress is decided by the Central Executive Committee (often its Standing Committee), and that of the Central Executive Committee by its Standing Committee. The Standing Committee has complete control, and may decide whether or not to have a Congress or a plenary session of the Central Executive Committee, and if so, when.

The Central Executive Committee has abdicated in favor of the Standing Committee. For practical purposes, the Standing Committee of the Central Executive Committee controls the party. This was certainly the case before the creation of the post of the Party Leader in 1938.

The Standing Committee used to meet on a fixed day of the week to transact whatever business the party needed to transact. Though, unlike the Congress and the Central Executive Committee, it was never given full powers, its authority was practically unlimited. It could even modify the resolutions passed by the Congress or the Central Executive Committee in a plenary session. Whereas the larger bodies could only resolve, the Standing Committee can also make appointments and issue orders. The advantages it had over them are obvious.

However, as the size of the Standing Committee grew, it also lost its effectiveness as an organ. Originally there were only eight members, but in 1945 the number grew to fifty. As it became a miniature of the Central Executive Committee, it acquired the same impotence as the latter.

THE PARTY LEADER

In addition to this pyramid of congresses and executive and supervisory committees, the party has also had a Leader since 1938. During his lifetime, Sun Yat-sen had always considered himself head of the party. He was Tsung-li, meaning General Manager, or President. There was, of course, nothing extraordinary in this, for the party, be it the Hsing Chung Hui, the T'ung Meng Hui, the Chinese Revolutionary Party, or the Kuomintang, was his organization. When the party was reorganized in 1924, he again assumed the title of Tsung-li. After his death the Second Congress of the Kuomintang in 1926 decided to retain in the Party Statute the provisions concerning this office with the declaration that to do him honor and reverence, Sun Yat-sen, the "Founder of the Kuomintang" should always remain President of the Party, though the presidential functions were to devolve on the Central Executive Committee. Under this arrangement it was naturally difficult for anybody to aspire to be the sole leader of the party; to do so would run counter to that spirit of reverence.

Moreover, there was only one man who wielded enough actual power to assume the high post of command, Chiang Kai-shek. But the senior leaders of the party were loath to see a man younger both in age and in party affiliation rise to inherit the position of Sun Yat-sen who had often lectured to them like an elder of the family. The question of restoring the post of leader thus remained moot for many years. Even as late as 1935, at the Fifth Congress, the Kwangtung and Kwangsi group of delegates, who generally considered Hu Han-min the senior leader of the party, threatened to bolt the sessions if the followers of Chiang Kai-shek dared to press for the restoration of the post. By 1938, however, the situation had greatly changed. There was a war going on. The whole country, even more than the whole party, was disposed to favor increasing the power and prestige of their commander-in-chief. Hu Han-min was dead. And in the face of the war, Wang Ching-wei could hardly interpose objection to the enhancement of the commander's position in the party. The Extraordinary Party Congress amended the Statute of the Party, established the office of Tsung-ts'ai, and elected Chiang Kai-shek to the post.

Tsung-ts'ai, meaning General Director, or Leader, is to be distinguished from Tsung-li, forever reserved for Sun Yat-sen. The Congress, in order to be meticulously correct towards Sun Yat-sen as Tsung-li, even went so far as to differentiate between the powers of the two posts: While the Tsung-li possesses the powers of high command, the Tsung-ts'ai merely exercises in the Tsung-li's absence the powers reserved for the latter. In other words, the party could say that it is the Tsung-li alone who has the powers of command. Of course, these were pure literary niceties for which the Chinese have a great weakness. The new Leader—namely, the Tsung-ts'ai— was henceforth to be the head of the party in name as well as in fact.

Chiang Kai-shek was elected Leader by the Congress in 1938. There is no provision in the Party Statute regarding the term of office. Presumably, the Leader continues in office until the Congress either abolishes the office or elects a new incumbent. At the following Party Congress, the Sixth, held in Chungking in May 1945, there was a difference of opinion as to whether Chiang Kai-shek should or should not seek a new mandate, or, more correctly, a confirmation. When Chiang Kai-shek tendered his resignation, the Congress at once unanimously resolved that he should continue as the Leader.

The restoration of a supreme head also posed the question of the party's repository of power. The theory that the supreme power was vested in the National Congress, and, after its adjournment, in the Central Executive Committee, was made no longer tenable. The Leader possesses an absolute veto over the decisions of the Central Executive Committee, and a suspensive veto over those of the Congress itself. If he disagrees with any decision of the Congress, he can ask them to reconsider. Then, he also presides over the meetings of the Standing Committee and there he controls all decisions made in the name of the party. As Leader of the Party, Chiang Kai-shek was given in 1938, according to the Statute of the Party, full powers, which he still enjoys.

Chiang Kai-shek is a man of strong will, fortified by an unusual amount of shrewdness and tenacity. Yet he is totally devoid of that quality of progressivism which saved Sun Yat-sen from prizing power for power's sake. A conservative by instinct, Chiang Kai-shek has no feeling of the spirit of the times. His lack of intimate contact with people of enlightenment, not to say common people, further deprives him of an opportunity to grow. The Actonian axiom, power corrupts and absolute power corrupts absolutely, is illustrated with devastating effect in his relationship with other men. In his anxiety to cling to power, more and more he mistrusts people who criticize him or even dare to differ with him. The men who work with him have to be first and last loyal to him personally. In the end he became the leader of a party of servile men but not a party of men and ideas, which were once the glory of the Reorganized Kuomintang.

DEMOCRATIC CENTRALISM

Like the Russian Communist Party, the organizational principle of the Kuomintang has always been in theory what is known as "democratic centralism." An orthodox interpretation of the term is that members have the rights of discussion, but when decisions have been made, they are to be obeyed by the dissenting members as well.

But the term came to be applied not so much to the making and carrying out of a party decision as to the mode of election of the party authorities and the power these elected authorities were to enjoy. According to the principle, the authorities were to be democratically elected by the membership, either directly by the party members themselves, or indirectly through intervening congresses, and, once elected, they were to have the powers of command and the right to be obeyed. Thus, the high authorities, in former years the Central Executive Committee or its Standing Committee, and since 1938 the Leader of the Party, have had the powers of direction and discipline over both the lower organization and the members; but since both the Committee and the Leader are elected, they can claim that they derive their supreme authority from the will of the members of the party.

In practice, however, "democratic centralism" can be democratic only when, in the process of organizing and electing, the members enjoy the right of forming minority groups, both to criticize the incumbents and to nominate candidates in opposition to the organization candidates. But that has not been the case. In the past the Provincial Executive Committees have more often been appointed by the Central Executive Committee than elected by the Provincial Congresses. The dominant group of the Central Executive Committee have therefore always been able to control the delegates to the National Congress and this in turn enabled them to perpetuate their own group in power. The established practice has thus become that whoever controls the Central Organization controls the party. There has been plenty of centralism but little democracy.

It is here that the hierarchy of party organization enters into the picture of party politics and strife. The dominant group may control all the organizations of the civilian party members. But the army organizations have always remained in the hands of a group of army politicians. The delegates sent by these latter organizations to the National Party Congress are naturally also from the army. They form a compact group. They obey the Leader who has been concurrently their supreme commander, but they need not submit themselves to or take orders from any civilian group, however powerful it may be. Within the hierarchy of army organizations, too, there is concentration of power to the exclusion of democracy. But in the party as a whole there cannot be monopoly of power either by a dominant civilian group or the army group. Whatever centralism there is is lodged in the hands of the Leader. Except in his case, neither part of the organizational principle of "democratic centralism" can be said to be in full operation.

PARTY ADMINISTRATION

Again like the Russian Communist Party, the organization of the Kuomintang does not end with the congresses and the executive and supervisory committees. At each tier there are a party secretary (always euphoniously titled) and a host of departments and commissions, appointed by the executive committee and responsible to it for their several administrations. The secretary occupies an important post, but not as important as that occupied by his opposite number in Russia. The number and the organization of these departments and commissions have varied greatly from time to time.

Of all departments, the Organization Department, having charge of the organization of the party branches below it, is naturally the most powerful. It picks delegates to the congress. It makes and unmakes the executive committees on the lower levels. It controls the membership, and consquently their votes. Its control is helped by the party secret service, innocuously called the Bureau of Investigation and Statistics, which keeps an eye on the thoughts and activities of the people outside as well as inside the party. It is correct to say that whoever controls the Organization Department controls the party. In fact, ever since the days of the split with the communists in 1927, a single group of persons has been in more or less full control of the Central Organization Department, all attempts to dislodge them having had no success. From the point of view of this group it is indeed a misfortune that they have not been able to control the organization of the party in the armies as well.

In addition, there have usually been departments for publicity and training, and also special units to cater to the special cadres of party members. These organizations are ordinarily more elaborate in the Central Party Headquarters and less so in the provincial or *hsien* party headquarters. They are often large establishments comparable in size and importance to the ministries of the Central Government or the administrative departments and bureaus of the Provincial and *Hsien* Governments. . . .

In theory the functions of the party departments are strictly party in nature. But during the days of tutelage of the Kuomintang, the government and the party never had a clear line of demarcation, either in function or in personnel. The result was, of course, constant interference in the affairs of the government and the actual exercise of governing powers over the people in general by these party departments.

The assumption of governing authority by party departments and the bureaucratic manner in which these departments are organized and in which the officials function have tended to bureaucratize the party institutions. Had the party been careful not to go over into the fields of ordinary administration and satisfied itself with merely giving directives to the Central Government which it had set up, it might have been able to preserve a spirit of vigilance and a vision of the future. It might have avoided creating so many bureaus and consequently converting so many party members into party bureaucrats who depend on the party for a living. A bureaucracy that has few functions to perform but is dependent on the office for a living always demoralizes the body politic which it serves. It is a calamity for the Kuomintang that it should have tolerated or even encouraged, perhaps unwittingly, the rise of one of the most idle and spineless bureaucracies China has yet had. . . .

SEGMENTATION WITHIN THE PARTY

Long before the appearance and disappearance of the Youth Corps, segmentation of the Kuomintang had been in the making. In an earlier chapter we have seen the various groupings competing with Chiang Kai-shek for control of the party. When Chiang Kai-shek became its undisputed leader, the process of segmentation continued.

The explanation for the existence of groups is to be sought in the nature of Chiang Kai-shek's leadership. He demands loyalty to his person. Having no conviction regarding any fixed policy and entertaining few fixed policies for any length of time, Chiang Kai-shek has naturally a tendency to consider his personal views of the moment to be best calculated to promote the interests of the nation and incidentally to be the most correct interpretation of Sun Yat-sen's ideas. He has deep faith in himself as the guardian angel of both the party and the nation. The convenient identification of his personal views with those of the party and the people and of his personal interest with the interest of the party and the nation also caused him to confuse individuals' personal loyalties with their party and national loyalties. As long as a man or a group of men remain loyal to him and do his bidding, he will extend his protection. Two groups of his loyal followers may differ from each other in ideas and policies, but it does not follow that therefore one of the groups must also have differences with him. Groups with irreconcilable ideas and policies either entertain no difference with his own views, ideas, and policies, or, if they do, they can relegate the differences to the background in order to give him unqualified support.

To illustrate: In the years immediately before the war in 1937, the groups which loyally supported Chiang Kai-shek did have differences in their attitudes toward the Japanese. Some favored a Fabian policy, nay, a policy of appeasement. Some were anxious to pick up the gauntlet of resistance. But since Chiang Kai-shek was the all-wise as well as the all-powerful leader and therefore must be combining the spirit of resistance and the unerring intuitions of a tactician, neither of the opposing groups could find objections to the views he entertained. Thus it was possible for both to support Chiang Kai-shek, though in the meantime they struggled against each other for an increased ascendancy in the councils of both the party and the government.

The Kuomintang groups which support Chiang Kai-shek have been numerous and shifting. The groupings are not strictly organized. They are illegal, for on the proposal of Chiang Kai-shek the Extraordinary Congress in March 1938 ordered all sectarian organizations to dissolve. That prohibition still stands. Therefore, though one hears often that so-and-so belongs to this group, and so-and-so is opposed to that group, it is not always easy to prove or to disprove the correctness of such an assertion.

In general, it may be said that among the supporters of Chiang Kai-shek there are three main groups. Small groupings also exist, but their influence is largely derived from the peculiar personal position of their leaders. They have no large followings and no ramifications. They usually ally themselves with one of the three. They have no chance to compete with any of the three for control of power either in the party or in the government.

Of the three, the most powerful is the Organization Group. Tracing its beginnings back to 1926, it has had an almost continuous hold on the Organization Department of the party. Having control of the party organization, it has been able to assume the pivotal position in both the party and the government, and thus enormously to expand its influence and increase its strength like an octopus.

The group is led by men who when still young fought the communists at the time of the split, understood the techniques of the Russian Revolution, and are prone to give a high evaluation, sometimes too high, to those techniques. But having fought the communists, they have acquired deep anticommunist and anti-Soviet convictions and prejudices. They have none of the literati tradition at all, though they take great pains to glorify the old in China. Some of them may make a great ballyhoo about Confucianism, but they do so only to echo some of Sun Yat-sen's dicta. They may be still feigning to be especially devoted to Min-sheng-ism. But their anticommunist obsession and their inability to draw really decent men of ability and honesty into their ranks has tended to make of the group machine-politicians solely intent on grabbing power, but without any idea of promoting the national interest.

Second, there is the Army Group. It consists almost wholly of the graduates of the Whampoa Military Academy. Its leaders have always adopted politics as their profession rather than active military command. The armies, certainly those units of which the Whampoa graduates have sole or even partial control, are the strongholds of the group. During the last years of the separate existence of the Youth Corps, their influence there was also predominant. They are now competing with the first group for hegemony in the Central Organization of the party.

The Army Group, though it has been carrying on an incessant struggle against the leadership and methods of the Organization Group, and has oftentimes been outspokenly critical, has very much the same outlook and tendencies in regard to the aims of the party and the ways in which the party should fulfill those aims. The members are strongly anticommunist and anti-Soviet. They also consider themselves revolutionaries and are not averse to using extralegal or even rather violent methods to achieve their purposes. They are opposed to the modern business and capitalist interests. In recent years they have directed some of their most violent tirades against what is known as bureaucratic capitalism, meaning officials accumulating fortunes by making use of their influence and position, though high army leaders themselves are not free from the selfsame practices.

Both the Organization and the Army Groups, or at least their younger leaders who have not yet acquired vested proprietary interests, are radical in their ideals for the economic rejuvenation of the nation. Both groups are extremely nationalistic in regard to encroachments on China's rights from without and intolerant of the demands of the minor nationalities within the borders of China. Regrettably, both have a low and unfavorable view of the Western democracies and are likely to stress Sun Yat-sen's second Principle, that of People's Power, interpreted as they understand it or like to have it understood—namely, an all-powerful government checked by none.

The third group, generally known as the Political Study Group, is not a party group, strictly speaking, though their leaders have been made members of the party's Central Committees. They had no chance to compete for the control of the party's machine with either of the two groups described above. Instead, they interested themselves in increasing their hold on the provincial administration and also on the larger financial and business concerns of the country, whether private or government. In other words, if the Kuomintang

Government and the Kuomintang are considered as different entities, this third group does not enter into the segmentation of the
party. But if they are considered inseparable entities, this group is
certainly next in importance to the other two.

The Political Study Group is quite distinguishable from the
other two. Being led by men of greater maturity both in age and
experience than the leaders of the other two groups, it tends to be
opportunistic or practical. To those who loathe dogmas, it seems
to be practical. To those who are allergic to plasticity, it seems to be
opportunistic. Whether one likes the group or not, its motto is to
ameliorate rather than to reform. It entertains no visions. It eschews
violence. Since many of the leaders of this group are themselves
men of wide financial and business interests, their views about the
necessity of economic readjustment are naturally mild. Likewise,
they are less nationalistic and somewhat more tolerant of the
democratic spirit of the West.

All groups, including minor ones, covet the control of the com-
manding posts in government and in business as well as of the
party machine. Since the Political Study Group has no hold on the
party organization, the competition is between the two other main
groups. In general, the Army Group controls the party organizations
in the army and the Organization Group controls the civilian
organizations of the party hierarchy. The civilian organizations
being more numerous, the Organization Group can control a
majority or something approaching a majority of the Party Congress,
and through it a majority of the Central Executive Committee.
That in fact has been the case during the more recent congresses.
But the Army Group in alliance with the others who are opposed to
the Organization Group is sometimes able to put up a stiff front
against the dominant group. If an impasse is occasioned by some
such rivalry, the Leader usually comes in to effect a kind of compromise, thus making himself indispensable to all.

The existence of two parallel secret services is the result of the
existence of several groups in keen rivalry to each other, but all
owing allegiance to one supreme leader. The Organization Group
controls the party secret service. The Army Group has an army
secret service ready to do its bidding. The two rival services may
come into conflict. But pluralism has its rewards for the leader who
can get reports on what he considers disloyal elements and at the
same time use the service of one group to check on the activities of
the other.

Outside of the party hierarchy the three groups have had different strongholds. The armed forces are of course the Army Group's exclusive sphere of influence. The party departments on various levels are similarly identified with the Organization Group. The latter group has also succeeded in controlling the schools, the civic bodies, the trade unions, and several very special branches of the civil service. The third group has several provincial administrations, and some banking and business concerns under their control. Lately all three have been racing for a share in local government, both on the provincial and on the lower levels. The growing interest of the Organization Group in banking and industrial enterprises and the interest of the Army Group in making some inroads into university circles seem to have been creating a confusion of the erstwhile distinguishable spheres of influence.

In a country with a more established order, such groupings as have just been described would perhaps be more naturally divisible into a radical and a conservative party, or if the Kuomintang had to remain as the sole party, into two wings. But the Kuomintang has a Leader who leads all groups and is not averse to seeing the party rent into groups so long as they are unquestionably and intimately loyal to him. There is an advantage in having these groups. Since the leaders of one group cannot exact loyalty from those of another, the leaders of all groups must take orders from him. A groupless Kuomintang is bound to develop one or more leaders who, though under the Leader, are yet above others. The position and influence of such men might acquire threatening proportions. It is true that Chiang Kai-shek did order the dissolution of all sectarian organizations or cliques in the party, in 1938; and, in a resolution on organizational principles of the party, passed by the joint session of the Central Executive Committees of the party and the corps, in September 1947, the sectarian organizations were again repeatedly derided and prohibited. But it would be fantastic to presume that he is unaware of the existence of the groups which, though lacking in emblems and official headquarters, are yet operating entities.

It is then clear that the Leader of the Kuomintang is not only the head of its organization, but actually holds it together. Or, to state it in another way, the Leader has allowed the party to be segmented so that he alone supplies the link between its several segments. It is in this all-important feature, rather than in its doctrine, or in its organization, or even in the social basis of its membership, that one can discover a key to the understanding of the Kuomintang.

7

PEKING'S RECOGNITION OF CRISIS

H. F. Schurmann

For some time now world interest in Communist affairs has been so centered in policy differences between Moscow and Peking that scant attention has been paid to the development within Communist China of a new crisis of far-reaching proportions. The crisis is essentially economic and seems to reflect, in large measure, the failure of the policies and methods initiated with such fanfare in 1958 under the banner of the "Great Leap Forward." Its result has been to force the Peking regime into a further retreat from the policies of the Leap—a retreat which, in fact, appears tantamount to a major shift affecting not only matters of basic economic policy but also the organizational role of the party. The crisis has also had significant repercussions in other areas, especially that of public morale. The present article, after briefly summarizing the main aspects of the crisis, will discuss the basic concepts which underlay the Great Leap Forward and then examine the latest policy changes and their implications. . . .

NATURE OF THE CRISIS

The present crisis thus has three main aspects: (1) an acute nationwide shortage of food caused by a combination of natural

Dr. Schurmann, Associate Professor of Sociology and History at the University of California, Berkeley, has spent considerable time in Hong Kong studying the problems of ideology and political organization in Communist China. In addition to the many articles on Communist China that he has published in recent years, Professor Schurmann is the author of *Economic Structure of the Yuan Dynasty* (1956) and other studies of traditional Chinese history. The present article is reprinted with the permission of the United States Information Agency, from *Problems of Communism*, Vol. 10, No. 5 (September–October 1961), 5-14. Minor deletions have been made in the text.

disasters and the disruptive effect of the policies of the Leap on agriculture; (2) major deficiencies in industry resulting from raw-material shortages, transportation difficulties, excessive emphasis on quantitative increases in production at the expense of quality, and general lack of coordination and careful planning; and (3) a serious slackening of effort and sense of commitment on the part of the peasantry and the intellectuals.

BASIC CONCEPTS OF THE GREAT LEAP

It is not generally realized that Communist China's second Five-Year Plan, which set the course to become known as the Great Leap Forward, inaugurated a pattern of development at considerable variance with that of the first Five-Year Plan and which deviated sharply, in its organizational concepts, from the Soviet model. The basic organizational ideas of the first Five-Year Plan had largely been straight borrowings from the USSR. This was a matter not of choice but of necessity, for the center of gravity of Chinese economic development lay in Manchuria, where Soviet influence and the regional power of Kao Kang brought into being a system hardly different from that of the USSR. Thus, the first Five-Year Plan concentrated on heavy industry, which meant that economic development was pushed most vigorously in a few favored regions, particularly Manchuria. Great bureaucratic and technocratic structures arose, characterized by rigorous centralism. Detailed centralized planning was emphasized. The dominant principle of industrial management was the Soviet "single-director system," which gave considerable weight to the economic bureaucracy, with a consequent diminution of the power of the local party committees in certain areas. That the committees must not interfere in managerial functions was a common admonition in those days. Land reform and a measure of "cooperativization" were carried out in China's vast agricultural areas, but the basic policy, as in the USSR, was to treat agriculture simply as a source of capital accumulation for industrial development.

Paradoxically, at the very time that Peking achieved centralization of the state apparatus in 1954, a counter-process started to shift decision-making power back to the party organs. As early as February 1954, the Fourth Plenum called for strengthening the role of the party committees in all basic-level organizations. With the announcement of the elimination of the Kao-Jao "antiparty group" in

March 1955, the policy of reinforcing the party's leadership at all levels intensified. The Eighth Party Congress of September 1956 marked the end of one organizational period and the beginning of a new one.

The new policy was "the mass line." Concretely, this meant several things. Excessively detailed and centralized planning was to be abandoned in favor of greater decision-making autonomy at the lower levels. The earlier policy of unequal regional development was to be replaced by one of simultaneous development of all areas of China; the entire society was to participate in the economic and social revolution. The role of manipulative leadership in this vast process was to devolve entirely on the party, which would wield supreme authority in all organized units. The Soviet "single-director system" was explicitly rejected in favor of "factory-director responsibility under the collective leadership of the party committee." All major decisions affecting economic enterprises were to be made by the party committees, and not by management alone.

Late in 1957, this process was carried a step farther by a series of decrees effecting a far-reaching decentralization of decision-making functions in industry, commerce, and finance. Lower-echelon economic functionaries acquired wide powers to modify and alter plans within loosely defined limits. Naturally, this meant increased power for the party committees, which held decisive authority at the unit enterprise level. *Ch'üanli hsiafang*—downward transfer of authority —was the slogan of the time. Indeed, it became a continuing movement, for from then until the end of 1960 there was a steady reduction and dispersion of administrative staffs. Central government functionaries were transferred to the provinces, administrative personnel to the production line, city cadres to the countryside. Around the same time articles appeared expounding the idea of "integrated economic regions"—*chingchi hsiehtso-ch'ü*. It was suggested that China be divided into seven such regions, each with its own basic industrial and communications structure, and there was even talk of creating integrated economic units at the sub-provincial level.

In sum, the organizational development which preceded the Great Leap was marked by two basic tendencies: (1) a massive strengthening of the party's leadership functions throughout the system as a whole; and (2) a gradual decentralization of economic decision-making authority to the lower-echelon units.

If the first Five-Year Plan period had essentially been one of imitation of the Soviet model, the second saw the Chinese Communists embark on their own "road to socialism" employing their own organizational methods. The new organizational approach called for the activation of basic-level organizations through the nuclei of party and activist groups rather than bureaucratic manipulation from the center, which for the most part has been the Soviet method. Herein lay the real significance of "the mass line": The pendulum swung from an essentially Soviet *modus operandi* of "centralism" to an essentially Chinese one of "democracy" (*i.e.*, mass action).

These developments set the stage for the Great Leap Forward and the introduction of the communes. The rejection of excessive, centralized planning—symbolized by Li Fu-ch'un's declaration at the Eighth Party Congress that "we must overcome the fault of watching too much and too tightly"—was to open the way for basic-level economic units to plunge forward, "setting targets, breaking them, and setting them again." Leadership was to be exercised by the party through its committees in industry rather than by the economic bureaucracy. The build-up of rural party cadres, enhanced by the *hsiafang* of great numbers of urban cadres to the villages, created the organizational basis for initiating a vast "mass-level movement." The dynamic nucleus of the economic effort was to lie in the basic units, and even more so in the smallest work teams. Each unit and each team was to be led by dedicated party cadres with full authority over its members and considerable power to make autonomous decisions in the interest of the rapid achievement of targets.

The general outlines of the Great Leap are well known. New industries sprang up throughout China, often in areas where rational planning would have discouraged capital investment. The "backyard steel" campaign was accompanied by an intensified work effort in established industries in order to over-fulfill each progressively higher set of production targets. In education, pure learning was abandoned in favor of a policy of "half study, half work." But the most far-reaching changes came in the countryside.

THE GREAT LEAP FORWARD

The communes provided the framework for the revolution in agriculture. There is no evidence that the Central Committee specifically planned the form that they should take, but the concept of enlarged agricultural units was essentially in line with an earlier, though only fragmentary, policy of "combining cooperatives" (*ping-she*), and the organizational changes just described laid the groundwork for their formation. They developed as integrated economic units, and with the establishment of commune industries, commune banking facilities, commune schools and hospitals, and commune militia, they tended in many respects to become "little nations" (a term actually used to describe them at one time). Thus, on the national scale, they represented an extreme point in the process of functional decentralization. But within the communes themselves rigorous centralization prevailed. The commune party committees acquired enormous power to manipulate the members: One of the basic features was a centralized system of labor allocation in which commune members were organized in work teams and brigades and assigned wherever their services were required

The Great Leap Forward was characterized, above all, by the "mass movement." Meetings of work brigades, teams, and other small groups at the base level were held constantly. Party cadres— who by this time held most of the leadership positions right down to the nuclear units—spurred the masses on to ever greater effort. It was a period of work and more work, of frenzy, and of confidence. The production figures announced late in 1958 for both industry and agriculture seemed to confirm the party's theory that the "mass line" could unleash vast new productive forces. After all, labor was China's most abundant asset, and the party seemed to have discovered a device by which it could be brought to bear on the economy on a more massive scale than ever before. The mainland press constantly talked of the crucial importance of leadership, not so much at the higher echelons as at the level of the production brigades and teams. Right up to the end of 1960, press reports continued to announce transfers of cadres from the higher administrative rungs down to the level of the basic working units.

Even before the end of 1958, however, there were signs that the Peking leadership was becoming concerned over the excesses of the Great Leap and the "communization" program. Initial modifications of the commune system were announced following the Sixth Plenum late that year, and early in 1959 an enlarged meeting of the Politburo at Chengchow adopted the so-called "three-level system of ownership" as the basic principle of commune organization, the effect of which was to curb the excessive centralization and egalitarian tendencies of the early days. The regime also took steps to remedy the breakdown in over-all coordination of the economy caused by the Leap, promulgating a new slogan of "the entire country a single chessboard." The subsequent discovery that 1958 crops had been far smaller than originally reported, supplemented by the losses inflicted on agriculture by the natural disasters of 1959, produced further repercussions. At the National People's Congress in the spring of 1960, Li Fu-ch'un enunciated a new policy of greater emphasis on agriculture as the basis of the national economy.

Yet, in spite of these evidences of concern, the regime continued to proclaim its confidence in the correctness of the "mass line." The somewhat obscure campaign against "right-wing tendencies" in the fall of 1959 apparently was aimed at those "planners" who had criticized the recklessness of the Leap. And all through 1960, writers in mainland publications continued to extol the organizational methods of the Leap and Mao Tse-tung's dialectical theories of "mass mobilization" in a tone of almost frenzied enthusiasm and optimism. The publication in September 1960 of the fourth volume of Mao's works, in which these methods and theories were expounded and sanctified as Chinese Communist orthodoxy, seemed to reaffirm the determination of the regime to persist on its existing course.

RETREAT IN THE COMMUNES

There is little doubt, however, that the Peking leadership, behind its public façade of confidence, was deeply preoccupied by the worsening economic crisis during 1960 and was, in fact, engaged in a soul-searching re-examination of its policies. This became quite evident when the central party organ *Jen-min jih-pao,* in two important editorials published on November 20 and 25, 1960, announced another major policy change affecting the communes. The effect of the new shift was virtually to do away with what had been initially one of the basic features of commune organization—namely, the centralized system of labor allocation.

Under the system as originally instituted in 1958, the commune as a whole had been the basic unit of operations. This meant that the commune administration was empowered not only to co-opt workers for construction projects such as waterworks and irrigation, but also to move them from village to village within the commune, wherever their labor might be needed. Given the Chinese peasant's traditional attachment to his own village, few aspects of commune policy had aroused such resentment as this. The system had already been modified early in 1959 by the adoption of the "three-level system of ownership," which made the production brigade rather than the whole commune the basic operational unit. While it lessened the degree of centralization, this change was only a partial retreat from the initial policy since, in practice, it was the large rather than the small production brigade which became the new basis of communal labor allocation.

To clarify further the practical effect of the 1959 revision as well as of the later change in November 1960, the two classes of production brigades must be differentiated more concretely. The large production brigade (LPB) has been described as "generally equivalent in scale to the original high-level agricultural producers' cooperatives," embracing anywhere from 200 (or slightly less) up to 300 households. Thus, each LPB would appear to correspond to a single large village or a group of smaller village communities. The small production brigade (SPB) is equivalent to the former "low-level" cooperative, consisting on the average of about 40 households, and thus corresponds to the typical small village community.

Whereas the revision of 1959 had shifted certain areas of administration from the commune to the LPB's, the new policy announced in November 1960 went a step farther to make the SPB the basic unit of operations. It also introduced a significant conceptual differentiation between rights of ownership and rights of use: Rights of ownership were vested in the LPB's, while rights of use—of labor, land, draught animals, farming tools, and equipment—were to accrue to the SPB's. The power of the LPB's to allocate labor and equipment of the SPB's was thus severely curtailed: Such allocations could thenceforth be made only with the consent of the SPB's. Furthermore, the new policy stipulated that "inasmuch as land-use rights have been assured the SPB, crop-planting rights must also be 'transferred downward' (*hsiafang*) to the SPB." Thus, although the LPB's would continue to decide general production plans and targets, the SPB's were to have the right, within these general limits, to operate as they thought best (*yinti chihyi*). In actual practice, as indicated by later reports, the LPB's fixed production targets in consultation with the SPB's, receiving "suggestions" from the latter and then trying to balance the suggested targets with "the needs of the state." The LPB also remained the basic unit for "unified accounting and unified distribution." The SPB's were required to deliver to the LPB their fixed production quotas as well as a certain percentage of any production in excess of the planned quotas; and the LPB handled the distribution of payments in cash and in kind to the SPB members. In short, aside from certain special tasks reserved to them, the LPB's became essentially an administrative unit in the commune structure.

While making these important internal changes, the November 1960 policy statement reunderlined the vital role of the communes themselves. The commune was to remain the basic-level unit of the state apparatus, as well as the primary unit of banking and financial activities. It would continue to operate any local industries established during the Great Leap and would remain responsible for basic construction projects (particularly irrigation and water works) and, presumably, for disaster relief. It also continued to be the base headquarters of the forces entrusted with maintaining internal security: that is, the militia and police.

Nevertheless, the new policy clearly spelled a basic change in the character of the communes. Whereas their function during the heyday of the "communization" drive had been essentially organizational, it had now become essentially administrative. Furthermore, as indicated later, there have been evidences of a change in the role of the cadres. Once something in the nature of minor military commanders, they are now being gradually transformed into administrators—an unhappy role for the party activist but one which the situation apparently has forced upon him. In a broader sense, the communes had originally been designed to create an organizational framework superseding the traditional Chinese village; but the November 1960 policy change recognized the failure of that attempt.

THE NEW GENERAL LINE

Up till the end of 1960, the successive revisions of policy announced by the Peking leadership had primarily concerned agriculture, but they were only the prelude to a more sweeping "across-the-board" shift embodied in the decisions of the Ninth Plenum of the Central Committee, which met in January 1961. Actually the Plenum, which lasted four days and was attended by 193 Central Committee members, took place not to make, but merely to announce, decisions already reached by the Politburo in December, on the heels of the Moscow conference of Communist Party representatives. The two main topics of discussion at the Politburo meeting had evidently been the Moscow conference results and policy for coping with the internal crisis. While one can only speculate concerning the influence of the former on the Politburo's domestic policy decisions, it seems highly possible that the isolation experienced by the Chinese Communists at the Moscow parley—and its implications for China's prospects of obtaining massive economic aid from the Soviet European bloc—may have been an important factor impelling the leadership to swing even more sharply away from "high speed" toward "balance" and "caution" in its internal policies.

As disclosed in the final communiqué summarizing its proceedings and decisions, the Plenum heard two major reports, one by CC Secretary General Teng Hsiao-p'ing on the Moscow conference and the other by State Planning Commission Chairman Li Fu-ch'un on the domestic situation and proposed policy changes. Li once again reaffirmed the leadership's confidence in the "three-sided red banner"—that is, the general line of socialist construction, the Great Leap Forward, and the commune system. He also pointed to considerable achievements in heavy industrial development during the first three years of the second Five-Year Plan, as a result of which, he claimed, the final production goals set by the plan for heavy industry had already been achieved.

With regard to agriculture, however, Li was much less encouraging. Although claiming great strides in irrigation, he acknowledged that the planned agricultural output targets for 1960 had not been fulfilled because of "serious natural disasters unprecedented for one hundred years." All efforts must be directed toward overcoming the difficulties in agriculture so as to assure adequate supplies of food and eliminate the shortages of agricultural raw materials for light industry. No new demands should be made on agriculture, and above all, since heavy industry had already achieved the second Five-Year Plan goals, the scope and speed of heavy industrial expansion should be reduced and emphasis placed instead on consolidation, quality of output, technological·improvements, and lowering of production costs. A revised draft economic plan for 1961, Li indicated, had already been prepared.

Li further took cognizance of a serious deterioration of public morale. Admitting the existence of dissatisfaction and a low level of political consciousness among party workers, he announced that a rectification movement was already under way, but that it would be carried out "by periods and by bits." There would also be a "cleansing" of party and public organizations. Finally, Li announced the establishment of six regional bureaus of the party Central Committee.

Although Li's statement was clear enough as to the general lines and objectives of Chinese Communist domestic policy in 1961, as usual it took some time for the full implications of the new policy, in terms of concrete methods and measures, to emerge in plainer view. Let us therefore examine the actual changes that have ensued in the three major sectors of industry, agriculture, and cultural-educational affairs.

SLOWDOWN IN INDUSTRY

Since the Ninth Plenum, there has been direct confirmation that the new policy spells a cutback in the projected rate of production increases in industry, together with a much greater emphasis on economy and efficiency of production, improved labor productivity, and technological advance. A retrenchment of production in the Wuhan Iron and Steel Company works has already provided concrete evidence of the slowdown in a crucial sector of heavy industry. The new line for industry has also been spelled out in greater detail by Po I-po, Chairman of the State Economic Commission and now also Director of the Office of Industry and Communications, in an important article published in *Hungch'i* (Red Flag).

Po's article made it clear that the keynote of industrial policy will be regularization rather than reckless expansion. Industry, he said, must lay major stress on improving the quality and variety of products; it must rely on increases in labor productivity, particularly through technological innovation, rather than on the recruitment of new labor; and to save materials and reduce production costs, there must be more effective management of output quotas and more careful cost accounting "by experts." Po stated that China had already created a "system of industrial management suitable for our country's circumstances," combining "tightly concentrated leadership with large-scale mass movements," but he also emphasized the necessity of raising the level of industrial management and adhering "rigorously to all rational operations systems, especially in the field of production technology." Above all, production must proceed in an orderly way: "If some sector or some unit deviates from the national plan, deviates from the needs of the whole, and one-sidedly develops its so-called 'positivism,' then this is not only harmful to the whole, but also harmful to that sector itself." To assure this, production must be run by "specialists" taking due account of actual conditions, and there must be rigorous efforts to "reform some comrades who are crudely unconcerned with detail, unwilling to understand, and often have no idea whatsoever of concrete conditions, but yet who direct production." Accordingly, said Po, a rectification movement would be carried out in all sectors of industry.

Subsequent articles in the mainland press have all borne out and elaborated the changes in Chinese Communist economic policy outlined by Po. In general, they reflect a return to centrally coordinated planning, orderly industrial management, and greater stress on technical rather than political competence. There is a renewed emphasis on "centralized leadership" and management "from the top down," rather than on large-scale mass movements "from the bottom up." "Political" leadership of production is being de-emphasized in favor of direction by "experts," and much stress is placed on strengthening managerial staffs concerned with administrative operations (planning, accounting, technological improvement, and so forth), the "system of responsibility," and the "orderly division of labor." As against the "high speed" of the Great Leap, the emphasis is now on "balance": The reckless setting, breaking and resetting of still higher output targets has been halted, and the idea of achieving rapid production expansion by group manipulation—which still prevailed in late 1960—appears to be giving way to a policy of inducing greater individual effort by means of material incentives. The new rectification movement is being directed toward curbing the dictatorial tendencies of work team leaders—usually party activists—who sometimes, as a recent press article put it, "are impetuous, resolve problems too simplistically, and do not sufficiently investigate and study."

All this indicates that the Mao-Liu theories of mass action, which were the ideological underpinning of the Great Leap Forward, have in effect been set aside even though no Chinese Communist spokesman has yet questioned the correctness of those theories or the "necessity" of the regime's resort to the policies of the Leap. The latter are simply regarded as a past phase of policy which has now been superseded by the new approach based on orderly planning and administration.

NEW COURSE IN THE COUNTRYSIDE

The shift of policy in agriculture has been even more far-reaching. As noted earlier, the new revisions of the commune system announced in November 1960 spelled, in effect, a return to a village-based rural economy. In addition, 1961 has seen the unfolding of a widespread rectification movement in the countryside aimed, as in industry, at curbing the dictatorial tendencies of the party cadres.

Despite restrictions on the outflow of mainland provincial newspapers (the chief source of information regarding developments in the countryside), Kwangtung papers reaching Hong Kong have carried extensive reports and articles which leave no doubt of the seriousness and thoroughness of the rural rectification drive. Moreover, occasional references to the campaign in the central press confirm that it is by no means limited to Kwangtung, and that the developments there may be taken as indicative of what is transpiring elsewhere in Communist China.

Numerous articles in the Kwangtung papers have been devoted to contrasting "right" and "wrong" methods of leadership, dividing the latter into two extreme tendencies—"hardness" and "softness." Since almost all the discussion has centered on criticism of "hard leadership," it is clear that this was the main problem. The culprits were in most cases young rural cadres who, it was charged, "did not understand conditions, did not study, and self-righteously carried out wrong policies." Whenever they met with opposition, they tried to force the masses to submit. "They would always shout . . . , 'An order issued must be obeyed!' . . . , and they would decree all kinds of punishments to assure such obedience and to preserve their so-called 'leadership prestige.' " The reports also spoke of rural mass meetings at which the cadres were denounced as a new elite, as men who in their arrogance had forgotten their social origins. "They no longer shared their lot with the masses; they sought leisure, worked little, ate much, spent a lot, received high rations, and became something special in contrast to the commune members."

The Kwangtung newspaper articles revealed, significantly, that the rural rectification movement has been organized by "party work brigades" (*kungtsotui*) similar to the special teams which fanned out years ago to carry out land reform. The use of this technique suggests that organization of the drive may have been one of the major tasks assigned to the regional bureaus of the party Central

Committee, the establishment of which was announced at the Ninth Plenum in January.

Rural rectification seems to have had two significant results. First, in the communes, it has reinforced the organizational decentralization effected under the November 1960 decisions by placing a relatively greater share of authority in the hands of the small production brigade cadres, who usually are the local village leaders. Frequent positive references in the press to "old peasants" testify to a restoration of authority to those at the village level with superior knowledge of local conditions. A second consequence seems to be a strenuous effort by the party to find new tasks for the rural cadres in place of the direct power they wielded in the heyday of "communization." Articles and broadcasts from the mainland constantly speak of the need "to investigate concrete conditions," "to compile statistics and data," to practice "orderly administration." All this suggests an attempt to transform the commune cadres— mostly young party activists who sprang to positions of leadership during the Great Leap—from little military commanders into competent administrators. This involves a shift of psychological perspective that is radical indeed.

But above all, the new line in agriculture spells a clear-cut and decisive triumph for the Chinese peasantry, with far-reaching social and political implications. It constitutes recognition by the regime that the only way out of the grave agricultural crisis lies not in increased pressures, but in concessions designed to stimulate the peasantry to renewed effort. Other recent developments all confirm this new approach. Thus, the earlier policy of excessive egalitarianism has been abandoned in favor of guaranteeing the more prosperous villages and harder-working peasants their gains. The Stakhanovite principle of "work more, earn more" has been universally adopted, although there has been some discussion whether work performance should be measured by the work-day or the quota system. The regime has also guaranteed that commune members shall receive a minimum of 70 per cent of production income in "wages." Much emphasis has been placed on fostering "supplemental household industries," especially the raising of domestic animals and garden crops.

A NEW BLOSSOMING?

Parallel with the far-reaching change of course in industry and agriculture, there has also been a shift in the attitude of the Peking

regime towards the intellectuals. Ever since the "antirightist" movement of 1957, the leadership had pursued a hard line towards the
group whose members, during the brief interlude of the "hundred
flowers" policy, had so grievously criticized not only its policies but
even the very substance of Communist party rule. The hard line
sought to correct the "individualistic" thinking of the intellectuals
by requiring them to perform periodic manual labor instead of
spending all their time "sitting in offices." Education was similarly
combined with work-training, and the new slogan of the day was
that everyone must become "red and expert," with rising emphasis
on "red."

In recent months, however, there have been multiplying evidences
of a turn away from these policies. In education, for example, an
article by the party secretary of Yünnan University, published in
Jen-min jih-pao (April 14, 1961), clearly signalled the abandonment
of the work-study policy. "A school is after all a school," declared the
author, who went on to state that there must be more concentration
on technical learning, that students must be given more time to
"digest" what they have studied, that courses and teaching methods
must be improved, and that the students' health must be preserved.
Mainland publications have been filled with articles on all kinds of
technical subjects, often starting off with the words "in my opinion.
. . ." So-called "meetings of immortals" (*shenhsienhui*) have been
organized throughout the country in an apparent effort to encourage
the intellectuals to speak their minds on a variety of issues.

There has also been a renewed emphasis in the Chinese Communist press on the "united front" and the need to cultivate the support of "nonparty cadres" and "democratic elements"—obviously a
bid to win over the intellectuals. Great stress has been placed on the
advancement of scientific work and raising the levels of education
and technology. Gone is the doctrinaire and fetishistic emphasis on
"manual labor," on "political" rather than "expert" leadership and
the *hsiafang* process which sought to assure it. Indeed, a new
"hundred flowers and hundred schools" movement has been officially proclaimed. Thus, if the concessions in agriculture represent
a victory for the peasantry, those in the cultural-educational sphere
mark a victory for China's stubborn intellectuals.

IMPLICATIONS AND OUTLOOK

All these shifts relate directly to the threefold crisis described at
the outset. The retreat in agriculture aims at resolving the critical

food situation through concessions to the much-abused peasantry; the renewed emphasis on centralized planning and rational management is designed to remedy the imbalances produced in industry and the economy generally by the haphazard haste of the Great Leap Forward; the relaxation of manipulative pressures in the cultural sphere is calculated to win back the support and cooperation of the disgruntled intellectuals.

Despite continuing talk about the "three-sided red banner," all these policy changes reflect a sharp swing away from the basic concepts of the Great Leap—a swing from mass manipulation to a limited degree of permissiveness; from decentralization to recentralization of organization on the national scale, but from centralization to decentralization of authority at the commune level; from exclusive emphasis on the party as the leader in all things to a greater reliance on expert direction of the economy; from egalitarianism to a policy of differentials and incentives; and, above all, from frenetic exuberance to cautious pragmatism ("all must proceed through experimentation").

The Chinese Communists now seem to be entering a third phase in their organizational development. As we have seen, the first phase was marked by considerable imitation of Soviet organizational methods and practices, while the second was characterized by a swing away from many of those methods in favor of a distinctive Chinese "road to socialism" concretely expressed in the policies of the Great Leap. In the new phase that is now unfolding, the Peking regime seems to be aiming at a balance between these two extremes. The swing would therefore seem to indicate a Chinese retreat toward Soviet concepts of the correct "road to socialism," but there is little doubt that hard economic realities within China, rather than any Soviet arguments, were the decisive factor in driving Peking to alter its course.

Can the new policies resolve China's internal crisis? No one, not even the Chinese leaders themselves, can yet hazard any judgment on that score. The most that can be said is that there is no sign at present either of a decisive breakdown of the system or of a decisive resolution of the crisis. The regime's system of organized controls itself remains intact. However, the policies of total control and total manipulation applied in the last few years have failed to bring about an economic breakthrough, and the regime is now hoping, through a relaxation of manipulative pressures, to evoke a renewed effort from China's overworked millions.

There seems good reason to believe that the internal socio-economic crisis is the overriding concern of the Peking regime. Toward that crisis the leadership has taken an approach of sober caution and pragmatism. Not only has stark reality deterred Peking from claiming further "triumphs of socialism," but the new approach is clearly one that does not lend itself to fanfare of the Great Leap variety. Perhaps the leadership is now groping about in an effort to put together a new party and organizational line to be presented at the Ninth Party Congress, which will have to take place in the not too distant future. In any case, in the face of the crisis and with no prospects of massive economic aid from the rest of the bloc, the Peking regime is moving with evident care and deliberation.

8

ECONOMIC CONDITIONS IN
THE LATE CH'ING PERIOD

Albert Feuerwerker

I
ECONOMIC THOUGHT

This is a subject which has not been adequately studied. . . .
The following, then, is perforce limited to a consideration of the
reformers and their quasi-economic programs. These are useful,
however, not merely because they are accessible. If the thinking of
these men was the most advanced of their time, it may be assumed
that it was inclusive of the outlook of those who undertook to
inaugurate enterprises modeled on the West. Therefore both the
insight and the naïveté which they reveal can illuminate the climate
of opinion into which the *kuan-tu shang-pan* industries were introduced.

Despite the burden of traditional terminology and probably
without being aware of the full significance of their insights, the
reform writers as a group were able to point to the most important
factors on which the successful economic transformation of China
would depend. No one writer was able to combine all these points
into a coherent program, nor was there any trace of systematic
theorizing. But the sum of their practical suggestions is evidence that

Dr. Feuerwerker is Professor of History and Director, Center for Chinese
Studies, The University of Michigan, Ann Arbor. In addition to the book
from which the present selection is reprinted, he is the author, with
S. Cheng, of *Chinese Communist Studies of Modern Chinese History* (1961)
and of articles on the history of modern China. Reprinted, with deletions,
with permission, from Chapter 2 of *China's Early Industrialization:
Sheng Hsuan-huai (1844-1916) and Mandarin Enterprise* (Cambridge:
Harvard University Press, 1958). Copyright © 1958 by the President and
Fellows of Harvard College.

the Chinese had at hand some of the same intellectual fuel, though they may not have been able to ignite it, which the Japanese used to propel themselves from an agrarian to an industrial society. . . .

To sum up this quick survey of reformist economic thought in the last decades of the Ch'ing dynasty: If, in fact, the Chinese merchant and official had been inspired with the same motivation as their Japanese peers, if there had been an agricultural surplus and if it could have been harnessed for the purposes of industrialization, if Chinese home industry had been able to win back the domestic market for manufactured consumption goods so as to obtain a secure base for further growth, if Western technology and organizational forms had been adopted on a scale and at a pace comparable to that of Japan, and if, finally, the Ch'ing government had been able to play a positive part in the realization of the foregoing program—if these five points of the reformers' economic proposals had been realizable, there is no question that the economic development of China would have assumed a far different form than that which is described in this study.

The insights which have been ascribed to the reformers were inadequate in several crucial respects. Most obvious is the fact that as a group these writers were not those who had the position and power to put their proposals into effect. Secondly, while they were in varying degrees aware of each of the key problems discussed above, their awareness was clouded by traditional terminology and naïve conceptions. They were not, after all, considering in retrospect the problem of why China's industry did not develop. To draw together their several insights into a more coherent whole than they themselves did is perhaps justifiable more on heuristic than on strictly historical grounds. In the third place, there were enormous gaps and misconceptions in their writings of which the following are examples: (1) there is no indication that they understood the structure of the traditional economy and the influence of traditional values as they affected the inadequate supply of capital for the new ventures they proposed; (2) they were weakest on the key question of the relation of agriculture to industrialization, showing no aware-' ness of the necessity for forced saving in agriculture as a basis for the initial growth of industry; (3) their understanding of the political situation—that is, the progressive decay of the Ch'ing governmental structure at least from the time of the Taiping Rebellion—was apparently limited by the closeness of events, for they assigned a major role to the state in the execution of their program.

II
GOVERNMENT FINANCE

It has been estimated that between 1868 and 1881 the Meiji government transferred over 34 million yen from current agricultural taxation into industrial investment. This amount was only 5½ per cent of the ordinary revenue for the period. But a better idea of its significance emerges from the fact that 34 million yen came to 13 per cent of government expenditure exclusive of the fixed costs of liquidating the Tokugawa regime, and that it amounted to over one third of the total outlay for the army and navy. And "significantly the first [government] bonds issued for public sale, in 1878, were to finance new industrial enterprise." Lockwood's study of the economic development of Japan has, I believe, done a service in correcting the common view that the remaking of Japan as an industrial power was entirely the work of the Meiji state. It nevertheless remains true that, especially in the early period, government effort and assistance were factors of supreme importance.

Moreover, even when the initial phase of direct government participation in the establishment of industrial enterprises had passed, the Meiji state made the largest contribution to the creation of the framework of communications and credit on which the growth of Japanese industry and commerce depended. This section is concerned with the financial inability of the Ch'ing government to follow the Japanese example and contribute directly or indirectly to the economic modernization of China.

Scholars who have examined the fiscal situation of the late Ch'ing period have tended to take the view that although the central government's financial position may have been deteriorating from the beginning of the Kuang-hsü reign (1875), it was only following the Sino-Japanese War of 1894-1895 that huge deficits which the government could not meet began to accumulate. After 1895 the triple pressure of indemnity payments, servicing foreign loans, and military expenditures totally wrecked the rough balance between income and outlay which Peking had maintained until that time. The increase in China's fiscal distress after 1895 is of course true, but unqualified emphasis on this point could lead to such extravagance as the following:

Before the Sino-Japanese War, China's finances were moving toward greater stability. The foreign debt was no more than several hundred thousand taels, and with the growing receipts from the maritime customs and the flourishing of *likin*, the government's finances were able to show an annual surplus. The founding of a navy, the building of railroads, the establishment of shipyards, and the inauguration of telegraph and telephone lines all were new undertakings which were based on the fiscal improvement of this period.

In fact, as Lo Yü-tung has shown, the annual surpluses reported by the Ministry of Revenue (*Hu-pu*) must have been illusory. Throughout the period from 1874 to 1894, the ministry was engaged in a series of largely unsuccessful efforts to raise funds in order to meet a continuing series of crises—the dispute over Ili with Russia, the Sino-French War, floods and famine, and the Sino-Japanese War. For emergencies such as Tso Tsung-t'ang's western expeditions and reconstruction in the northwest, the government was forced to depend on foreign borrowing. Before 1894 nine loans totaling Tls. 40,000,000 were made, mostly for defense and immediate needs. These funds came from foreign firms in the treaty ports, not from foreign governments. It is also a fact, however, that some Tls. 33,000,000 had been repaid on these loans before the Sino-Japanese War. This repayment is an indication that the problem was not merely the very real one of the inadequate resources of the Chinese economy as a whole. In large measure the financial straits in which the Peking government found itself were due to the decay of the fiscal institutions by means of which it could command such financial capacity as there was in its empire.

To suppress the Taiping Rebellion (1851-1864), Peking had been forced to grant a large measure of authority to leaders of gentry-official cliques, such as Tseng Kuo-fan and Li Hung-chang, who had organized the only Chinese forces able to contend with the rebels on equal terms. These new military leaders tended to dominate the key posts of governor-general and governor until the end of the century, marking not only a shift of power in the provinces from Manchus to Chinese but also an augmentation of the power and influence of the provincial governors-general and governors as against the imperial government in Peking. These local leaders tended to form regional "bases" or "machines," founded on the military forces they had organized against the Taipings, which were able to drive hard bargains with Peking. The clearest case of this development was that of Li Hung-chang, who with his Huai Army (*Huai-chün*) dominated northeastern China for almost a quarter of a century, until his army and navy were disastrously defeated by the Japanese in 1894.

The Taiping Rebellion was a fiscal as well as a political turning point for the Manchu dynasty. This change was symbolized by the eclipse of the provincial treasurer (*pu-cheng shih*) who had been the official in the provinces responsible to the Hu-pu for the taxes collected by the local magistrates. The new sources of taxation developed originally by the provincial leaders to support their campaigns against the Taipings were under the direct control of the governors-general and governors; only the traditional land and "miscellaneous" taxes continued to be administered by the provincial treasurer. Among the new revenue sources the most important was *likin,* which was first instituted in 1853 in Kiangsu as an internal transit tax on grain passing through the Grand Canal. By 1862 it had been applied to nearly all commodities and had been copied by every province except Yunnan, Heilungchiang, and Formosa. In some cases *likin* had come to be charged not only along the route of transit but also as a production tax at the point of origin and as a kind of sales tax at the destination .The rate varied widely, from 1 to 20 per cent *ad valorem.* The share of this new income that the provinces remitted to Peking was only a fraction of the annual yield, perhaps 20 per cent.

In a typical year in the last two decades of the nineteenth century, Peking's revenue from all sources was probably something like the estimate shown in Table 4. This total does not represent the actual

Table 4

Estimated Annual Revenue Reported to Peking

Land tax	Tls. 25,088,000
Grain tribute	6,562,000
Salt gabelle (including salt *likin* of approximately Tls. 7,500,000)	13,659,000
Likin	12,952,000
Maritime customs (1893)	21,989,000
Native customs	1,000,000
Duty and *likin* on native opium	2,229,000
Miscellaneous taxes, sale of office, "contributions," etc.	5,500,000
Total	Tls. 88,979,000

physical remittance of tax receipts to the capital. It is the amount reported yearly (in two installments) by the provinces to the Ministry of Revenue, which was then stored in money or in kind in the several provincial treasuries to await allocation by the ministry. Eventually one part of the reported total was retained by the province in question to cover local expenses for the ensuing period, a second portion was remitted to Peking (or elsewhere at the direction of the Hu-pu), and in some cases a third part was shipped as grants-in-aid to other provinces.

As already noted in the case of *likin,* the revenue reported annually to Peking was very far from being the same thing as the total tax collection of the empire. This theory was made more flagrantly fictitious by the developments that have just been described as following from the Taiping Rebellion, in particular the growing power of the provincial high officials vis-à-vis the imperial institution and the metropolitan bureaucracy. Whatever the potential fiscal resources of the country, the share which came under the control of the central government was largely inelastic. The quotas due from the land tax and grain tribute had been fixed since the Ch'ien-lung period (1736-1796). *Likin* and the native customs were in fact under the control of the governors-general and governors who were often able to resist demands from the Hu-pu for increased remittances on the plea that Peking was ignorant of the true financial situation in their provinces. The import tariff was fixed by international treaty, leaving only the salt gabelle and miscellaneous minor taxes which could to some extent be manipulated by the central government. H. B. Morse, for example, in a work published in 1908 offers the synthetic figure Tls. 284,154,000 as a grand total of "the amounts presumed to be paid by the taxpayer." Lo Yü-tung notes that according to the provincial *Ts'ai-cheng shuo-ming-shu* (Descriptions of financial administration), which are the reports of Financial Reorganization Bureaus set up by imperial decree in each of the provinces in 1909, the total revenue for 1908 (Kuang-hsü 34) came to more than Tls. 200,000,-000—twice the amount reported to Peking. The discrepancy between the totals suggested by Morse and Lo and the revenue actually reported to the central government represents that part of the financial capacity of the empire which was retained by local and provincial authorities either for legitimate needs or as part of the universal "squeeze" that characterized every financial transaction. Provincial retention of land-tax and *likin* collections made up by far the largest share of this amount; perhaps only 20-25 per cent of the revenue under these heads was reported to the capital.

For the sake of comparison, the Japanese land-tax revision of 1873 should be noted briefly. The Meiji oligarchs in their concern for stable government revenue saw that they must provide a unified system of taxation with a yield which would not fluctuate with the size of the harvest. Their basic scheme was a change from the diverse levies, usually in kind, which had been imposed arbitrarily or by custom by both the *Bakufu* and *han* governments, to a unified money tax under the direct control of the new central government. This tax was fixed at a uniform rate of three per cent of the land value, which in turn was assessed at 8.5 times the average annual crop yield. Its collection thus amounted to about 25-30 per cent of the annual crop value. At the outset the new land tax provided 94 per cent of the government's revenue, and it continued to account for over 50 per cent until almost the turn of the century. The key role of land-tax revision in the success of the Meiji reforms is summarized by E. H. Norman:

> The revision of the land tax was not a hasty make-shift measure but a reform which occupied the best minds in the government over a long period of time. . . . By providing for a *constant* source of revenue, they [the Meiji oligarchs] were making possible a modern budgetary financial system. In a country still agricultural and lacking tariff autonomy it was natural that the very considerable burden of military expenditures as well as of capital outlay for model industries and the maintenance of a large body of bureaucrats should be made dependent on the land tax, and it was important that this revenue should not fluctuate.

This demonstrated ability of the Meiji government to make the best possible use of the financial resources available to it stands in striking contrast to the difficulties of the Ch'ing government which we have outlined.

If the Ch'ing government was already a sufferer from financial disability before 1895, consider what the effects of the Sino-Japanese War and the Boxer Rebellion must have been. To repay the Russo-French and Anglo-German loans which were contracted in order to meet China's Tls. 230,000,000 indemnity to Japan, the Hu-pu was called upon to produce some Tls. 20,000,000 annually above its prewar outlay. From 1902, payments on the principal and interest of this debt, together with the Boxer indemnity payments, required more than Tls. 42,000,000 annually.

Whence did the funds come? In the case of the Russo-French loan of 1895 and the Anglo-German loan of the following year, payments were made from the maritime customs receipts. The supplementary Anglo-German loan of 1898 was also formally secured by the customs revenue. However, in order to meet the annual payment of Tls. 5,000,000 the Hu-pu was also obliged to pledge revenue from salt and *likin,* six collectorates in the Yangtze basin being placed under the supervision of the Inspectorate of Customs. This is only the beginning of the matter. The important problem is to determine from what sources the Hu-pu was able to raise funds with which to offset the deficit in its regular income resulting from the diversion of customs and *likin* receipts to the service of the foreign debt.

The answer in part lies in the steady increase of China's foreign trade which produced augmented customs and *likin* revenue. In the period 1871-1885, the average annual value of exports and imports together was Tls. 144,000,000. This average jumped 76 per cent, to Tls. 254,000,000, for the years 1885-1898. For 1899-1913 the annual average increased to Tls. 657,000,000. As they bear on the payment of foreign indebtedness, however, these figures must be qualified with the statement that in the same period the decline in the price of silver meant that some of the increased customs revenue was offset by the necessity to pay more taels per gold franc or pound. For the rest, Lo Yü-tung details a whole series of efforts by the Hu-pu to increase the yield from the traditional sources of revenue, but they seem to have produced very uncertain results. Provincial opposition to increased salt prices, to the reduction of salaries and emoluments, to higher tax quotas on native opium, and to increased central control of opium brokers was very strong, with the result that Peking's gains under these categories were small and temporary.

Of some interest was an attempt by the Hu-pu to float a domestic loan at the beginning of 1898. One hundred million taels of *Chao-hsin p'iao,* or "Sincerity Bonds," were to be marketed in Peking and the provinces. The bonds paid five per cent per annum and were redeemable in twenty years. This attempt at modern financing was unable to escape the fate of assimilation to the traditional practices of Ch'ing finance. In January 1899 an imperial edict stated:

Owing to the many cases of extortion complained of, arising from dishonest officials compelling people to subscribe to *Chao Hsin* Bonds we commanded that, with the exception of officials in the provinces and wealthy merchants and gentry who had already subscribed and paid for the said Bonds, no more canvassing was to be made among the gentry, traders, and masses, nor was payment to be forced from those who had subscribed but were unable to meet their obligations. In fact it was our intention to put a stop to any further sale of *Chao Hsin* Bonds. . . . Now we again issue this command to all. . . .

Probably no more than Tls. 10,000,000 of the bonds were sold.

Yet, for the payment of the Boxer indemnity, and in one other very different case which will be discussed later, the Peking government was able to compel the provinces to contribute very large sums above their customary quotas. Table 5 gives a breakdown of

Table 5

Sources of Boxer Indemnity Payments, 1902-1910

	Maritime customs	Provincial assessments	Hu-pu (Ministry of Revenue)	Total
Tls.	33,000,000	164,000,000	27,000,000	225,000,000
Per cent	16	72	12	100

the sources of the payments that were made on the Boxer indemnity for the nine years 1902-1910. Perhaps two thirds of the Tls. 33,000,000 obtained from customs receipts could be attributed to increased collections following from the 1902 tariff revision; the remainder for the most part came from the receipts of the native customs stations within fifty *li* of each treaty port which had been placed under the Inspectorate of Customs by the Boxer Protocol. The Hu-pu's annual contribution of Tls. 3,000,000 (Tls. 27,000,-000 for the nine years) was obtained by ceasing payments to certain old-style military units and by "temporarily" ending rice grants to Manchu and Chinese officials and to the Eight Banners. But the truly remarkable fact is that Peking was able to extract more than Tls. 18,000,000 annually (Tls. 164,000,000 for the nine years) from the provinces.

How was this done? We know that the provinces protested very strongly against the schedule of payments which the Hu-pu drew up for them. Five governors-general and eleven governors joined in a telegram to Peking in which they beseeched the "Imperial favor . . . that the throne permit the indemnity payments due from the provinces to be reduced by 30 per cent." But with the backing of Prince Ch'ing (I-k'uang), who had conducted the Boxer peace negotiations together with Li Hung-chang and had continued in charge of liaison with the foreign powers, the court stuck to its original position and ordered full payment of the assessments. The intervention of Prince Ch'ing supports the conclusion that the major threat which the court held over the provinces in order to force compliance with its demands for funds was that of possible foreign intervention if the Boxer payments were not met. While previous demands for funds had been more in the manner of negotiations, with the local authorities able to resist with some success, in this instance the central government was able to take a firmer stand. Provincial payments had to be deposited monthly in Shanghai, and there was no room allowed for bickering as to the amount. With one minor exception, the payments were made on schedule and in full.

Whence came these provincial funds—the annual quotas ranged from Tls. 2,500,000 each for Kiangsu and Szechwan to Tls. 200,000 for Kweichow? The chief sources were the land tax, an increase in the price of salt, and *likin*. That is, the provinces were required to remit funds under these categories in addition to their regular quotas as shown in Table 4 above. It is not clear to what extent this was accomplished by heavier taxation on the populace rather than by a diversion of Tls. 18,000,000 annually in existing revenues which had previously been outside of the control of the Peking government.

The fact that such a large sum could be raised, albeit in the very special circumstances of the occupation of North China by the Allied armies, invites comparison with the felicitous results to Japan of the 1873 land-tax revision. In a sense the Tls. 164,000,000 which the provinces paid regularly and in full over a nine-year period, and in addition to the customary taxation which they reported each year to Peking, was parallel to the increased resources which the Meiji government was able to command after it had reformed and centralized the land tax. Of course the differences were profound. In China the arrangements were makeshift and assimilated to the traditional fiscal structure; in Japan, the new revenue of the central government was the result of a conscious act of policy which had "occupied the best minds in the government over a long period of time." Of even greater immediate significance was the disparity in the uses to which these resources were put: for a modern army and the beginnings of modern industry in Japan; for the totally nonproductive payment of indemnities to foreign powers by

China. To state the matter in its darkest terms, the effect of the Tls. 164,000,000 in question was actually negatively productive inasmuch as these payments were a net loss to China's total available resources.

This comparison is not meant to imply that the economy of nineteenth-century China was potentially able to provide either the capital or the technology for rapid and extensive economic changes. But within the limits of what might have been done in the given circumstances, the question must be posed: If the Ch'ing government could exert enough pressure to force the provinces to remit the large sums that were required for the Boxer payments, why could it not act likewise to mobilize funds in order to carry out a program of military reform and pioneer industrialization? Among the impediments to such action was the decline of the effective power of the central government, which has already been noted. But this, after all, was only relative so long as the imperial system survived. The obstacles are made clearer by a second instance of successful money-raising. This was the "mission" of the grand secretary Kang-i.

In June 1899 Kang-i, later infamous as a sponsor of the Boxers, left Peking for a tour of the southern provinces with the purpose, according to the Peking correspondent of the *North-China Herald,* of raising Tls. 2,000,000 "to aid in filling up the Imperial Treasury." The grand secretary's attention was first directed to the *likin* collections, the salt gabelle, and the offices of the China Merchants' Company and Imperial Telegraph Administration in Shanghai. In all, he extracted some Tls. 1,200,000 from Kiangsu province before turning his attention to Kwangtung, where his reorganization of the *likin* collection was nominally to have produced Tls. 1,600,000 annually for the empress dowager's coffers.

Contemporary opinion in the treaty ports was uncertain as to the meaning of Kang-i's mission. Did his successful extraction of large sums from the provinces indicate that Tz'u-hsi and the Manchu conservatives had finally realized that "reform" was necessary, and were therefore seeking to centralize China's finances in an effort to make up the Tls. 20,000,000 annual deficit in Peking? Or was it that the empress dowager and her followers were seeking funds for their private purposes and to strengthen themselves against the reform party? This uncertainty is resolved when we consider that the leading victims of Kang-i's money-raising trip were the China Merchants' Steam Navigation Company and the Imperial Telegraph

Administration. These enterprises and a handful of others represented whatever there was of a modern sector in the Chinese economy, that sector which, in contrast to the crippling burden imposed by Chinese officialdom, the Meiji leaders were doing their utmost to foster in Japan. Despite Sheng Hsuan-huai's warning to the court that the Hanyang Ironworks, the P'ing-hsiang Coal Mines, the Huasheng Cotton Mill, and other modern enterprises which he headed were dependent on the China Merchants' Company and the Telegraph Administration, Kang-i forced Sheng to pledge at least Tls. 100,000 annually from these two companies as a "contribution" to the imperial treasury. Almost simultaneously, another grand secretary, Hsü T'ung, was proposing that the liquid assets of the China Merchants' Company, the Telegraph Administration, and the K'ai-p'ing Coal Mines be appropriated by the court on the grounds that they represented surpluses which should have been used "for the benefit of the government."

Thus even if the central government had been able to improve its financial position, it is unlikely that it was ideologically able to support an extensive program of economic modernization. Such enterprises as those that were the victims of Kang-i's mission were conceived of by the dominant political power as one more source of funds, analogous to additional *likin* stations or a higher price for salt. They were fiscal units always open to official exactions, rather than prototypes of a new and sought-for economic order. The vision necessary to carry out a fundamental transformation of society was all too absent in Peking as compared with Tokyo. ·

III

TRADE AND COMMERCE

Much of the discussion of the enormous contrast between the experience of China and Japan has centered on the alleged strategic differences in the role of the merchant in these two countries. For example, the relatively "open" class structure of China is contrasted with the "closed" class structure of Japan. The former allowed the wealthy merchant or his sons to rise into the gentry class by the purchase of land and rank or by competition in the civil service examinations. In Japan the merchant was forced to maintain his mercantile identity and, like the French bourgeoisie of 1789, became anxious to overthrow the Tokugawa feudal regime. The fact is, however, that a fundamental characteristic of the traditional merchant class in both Ch'ing China and Tokugawa Japan was its close and even parasitic relationship to the agrarian economy and indirectly to the conservative political structure.

In Japan, it is true that the *daimyō* and *samurai,* with the growth of a money economy in the Tokugawa period, became increasingly dependent on a merchant class to convert their feudal rice incomes into money. This is seen in the commercial relations which developed between the *samurai* and a class of rice brokers, the *fudasashi,* and in the growing importance of the *kuramoto,* the financial agents of the *daimyō* in Edo and Osaka. There were many instances in which the wealthier merchants became tied to *samurai* families by marriage or adoption. But the important fact to note for the present discussion is that the point at which the wealth and influence of these merchants was growing was precisely that point at which the *samurai* and *daimyō* were articulated to the Tokugawa feudal system. It was only after the Meiji government had replaced the collection of rice in kind by a uniform money tax, and had carried out the compulsory commutation of the *daimyō* and *samurai* pensions with which it had initially replaced their rice revenues, that the way was cleared for economic development in the direction of industrialization. These measures in fact must have had an untoward effect on the *chōnin* (the term generally applied to the merchant class during the Tokugawa period) who had been the commercial agents and the creditors of the feudal classes.

In the light of Japan's actual success in transforming her economy, these observations point, at least tentatively, to the conclusion that what was important in the situation of late Tokugawa Japan was not only the position occupied by the merchant class, but also the actual degree to which the economy had become commercialized. This subject still awaits adequate comparative study. But might it not have been the case that, despite the weakness and vulnerability of the merchant's position, the industrialization process of the Meiji period was facilitated by the prior development of a market orientation considerably in excess of that present in late Ch'ing China?

In traditional China the merchant was simultaneously devalued and needed. The low valuation of mercantile activity was in part a reflection of the role of commerce in an agricultural society in which the dominant values were those of the Confucian gentry-official. In essence it was the lack of development of the market—the inability of the peasant producers to effect an exchange of their products on any more than a parochial scale—which enabled the merchant to realize substantial profits. By taking advantage of local variations in market price to buy rice where it was cheap and to sell it dearly in areas of local famine, he drained from the peasant the surplus above the minimum needed for survival. At the same time, the merchant was competing for that surplus with the gentry-landlord, and with the entire official bureaucratic structure which was ultimately supported by taxation and multiple customary exactions on the total agricultural product. It followed that in the dominant ideology the merchant was seen as essentially parasitic on the two classes accorded the highest positions in the traditional rank-order of gentry-official, peasant, craftsman, merchant (*shih, nung, kung, shang*).

On the other hand, even in an underdeveloped economy, there were essential exchange operations, public and private, for which the merchant was indispensable. For example, despite the low prestige of business enterprise and the prohibitions against officials taking part in it, clandestine business relations between members of the bureaucracy and merchant associates in such fields as overseas trade and rice transport seem to have been a persisting practice. And, of course, the prevailing monetary system was dependent on the arbitrage of middlemen. We might also suggest that the traditional merchant—in addition to the commercial transactions of the kind already noted—functioned as part of a vast decentralized system akin to tax-farming, which characterized the financial structure of early modern China. How pervasive this institution was is revealed by recent studies of the *ya-hang* (brokers) system, the countrywide practice of licensing brokers by local officials to collect commercial and market taxes in the many hundred market centers of China.

The ties between the government bureaucracy and commercial enterprises are seen most clearly in the salt administration, perhaps the largest single economic enterprise in Ch'ing China. For example, in the lower Yangtze provinces (the Liang-Huai salt district, which was the most important of eleven in eighteenth-century China) the production of salt was dominated by some thirty "factory merchants" (*ch'ang-shang*) who owed their positions to government recognition. Distribution and sales were farmed out to an equal number of "transport merchants" (*yün-shang*) who had been able to pay the salt gabelle in advance and who received monopoly rights in designated areas. These large merchants and hundreds of smaller ones were part of an elaborate tax-farming institution which produced rich profits for themselves as well as revenue and "squeeze" for the court and the metropolitan and provincial bureaucracy. The annual aggregate profits of the transport and factory merchants of the Liang-Huai salt district alone have been estimated at between six and seven million taels (equal at the very least to the equivalent number of dollars). But despite the large capital involved in salt production and storage and the substantial profits that were realized, the salt merchants developed no distinctive bourgeois consciousness which would have set them apart from the traditional social structure. They definitely shared in the dominant values of the old order, and were not opposed to it even under the burden of official exactions which amounted to nearly Tls. 40,000,000 to the imperial treasury alone between 1738 and 1804. Their adherence to Confucian values, which include the subordination of purely economic motivation to considerations of kinship and status, is evident from the efforts of successful merchants to rise into the gentry class by putting their profits into land, purchasing official rank, and cultivating literature and art.

The obligation to assist less fortunate members of one's clan and the absence of primogeniture were further factors making for what in an economic sense was the dissipation of accumulated mercantile capital. Above all, the existence of monopoly profits depended on the continuation of the traditional fiscal system of the Ch'ing state and thus on the whole complex of conservative institutions of which these refractory finances were but one aspect. The traditional merchant, of whom the salt monopolist was a prime example, was as unable as the majority of the bureaucracy to play a positive part in developing China's economy. As one final consideration, it might be observed that their accumulations of capital were, after all, large only by the standards of an agrarian economy. The requirements of modern industry and communications could never have been met out of the proceeds of the salt gabelle even if those profits had been collected for that purpose.

If such was the inability of the traditional Chinese merchant, what of the new class of merchants, the "compradores" (*mai-pan*), who were a product of the development of commerce in the treaty ports after the Treaty of Nanking? Or, more broadly, if Chinese domestic commerce and trade were irrevocably linked to the old order, could more be expected from foreign commerce, which Lockwood has described as having had such a marvelous effect in Japan?

For Japan herself foreign commerce proved to be the key unlocking the door of economic opportunity. Initially it provided a highway over which new impulses and a new technology came to revolutionize much of her economic life. Later it enabled her to draw increasingly on the world's industrial resources to compensate for her own basic deficiencies. As a result she came to acquire a degree of dependence on the world economy exceeded by that of few other nations in modern times.

As I have shown in the first chapter, to some extent the *kuan-tu shang-pan* system was designed to tap "compradore capital," the accumulation of funds by Chinese merchants from foreign trade and its ancillary services in the treaty ports, first as employees of Western firms and later on their own account. Several former compradores, including Tong King-sing, Hsü Jun, and Cheng Kuanying, whose participation in the enterprises most closely associated with Sheng Hsuan-huai will be examined in the following chapters, played major roles in the earliest industrial undertakings. But these men, despite their participation in foreign trade, their residence in the treaty ports, and their association with foreigners, were never wholly free of the past. They were, in the first place, assimilated to the traditional official system, holding official rank and usually the title of expectant taotai. When Hsü Jun, for example, was cashiered in 1884 for misappropriation of China Merchants' Company funds, he held a "brevet rank of the second grade" and was an "expectant taotai in Chekiang." Hsü was greatly concerned to regain Li Hung-chang's favor, and finally in 1890, after he had repaid his defalcations in full, Li memorialized requesting that Hsü receive "the button of the third class" and be restored to the position of expectant taotai. Tong and Cheng of course also were expectant taotais.

Secondly, even those treaty-port merchants who also had a hand in modern industrial or financial enterprises were not exclusively occupied with such undertakings. Hsü Jun, while assistant manager and a large shareholder in the China Merchants' Company and an official of the K'ai-p'ing Coal Mines, made a fortune in real estate and the tea trade, more traditional objects of investment and speculation. When the Imperial Bank of China was opened in 1897, its first directors were leading merchants of Shanghai, including Yen Hsin-hou, originally of Chekiang and an expectant taotai. Yen operated "customs banks" (*hai-kuan kuan-yin-hao*) in Canton, Foochow, Shanghai, Hankow, and other treaty ports which he agreed to join to the modern-style bank that Sheng Hsuan-huai was inaugurating. The first Chinese manager of the new bank was Hsieh Lun-hui, who had operated an old-style "money banking shop" (*ch'ien-chuang*) in Shanghai. Although Yen, at least, in the next decade was the promoter of several industrial enterprises in Ningpo and in Kiangsu, it is hardly likely that the operations of the Imperial Bank escaped being influenced by the traditional background of its directors. This was the case, notwithstanding its regulations, which were patterned after the British-operated Hong Kong and Shanghai Banking Corporation. If men like Yen Hsin-hou and Hsieh Lun-hui, who were willing to back a modern-type bank, were themselves tinged with the old, many more refused the challenge of the new entirely. The example of Hu Kuang-yung, the silk merchant and customs banker who was instrumental in arranging China's earliest foreign loans, is a good one in this connection. He turned down Li Hung-chang's invitation in 1873 to participate in the financing and management of the China Merchants' Steam Navigation Company, which was being organized at that time.

Further, the inducement was small for those merchants who had accumulated funds from the export of tea and silk, the distribution of foreign imports, or from customs banking and the like to put their wealth into textile mills, shipping, or mines. On the one hand they were attracted by the prestige (and relative safety from official exactions) of owning land. The tendency for merchants to purchase land and fuse with the local gentry is implicit in the ubiquitous reference to the "gentry and merchants" (*shen-shang*) of such and such a locality in late nineteenth-century documents. Possibly in the chambers of commerce (*shang-hui*), such as that established in Shanghai by Sheng Hsuan-huai, the local merchants and gentry may have had a meeting place. On the other hand high returns could be realized from investing in usury, native banks, and pawnshops. The guaranteed interest (*kuan-li*) on shares in the China Merchants' Company and in the Hua-sheng Cotton Mill seems high at eight or ten per cent, but even this amount could not compete with the 20-50 per cent per annum which could be earned by traditional-type investments.

As to the effect of foreign commerce, more broadly considered, it may be argued that what took place in the treaty ports of the China coast differed qualitatively as well as quantitatively from developments in Japan. In fact, before the Sino-Japanese War the disparity between the degree of modern economic development in these two countries was not yet flagrant. Take the specific case of the import of machinery. For the years 1889-1893, Japanese imports of machinery, instruments, and vehicles totaled about 6,000,000 yen. In these five years China's machinery imports were valued at Tls. 3,181,000, approximately the same value as the Japanese total if we take one tael as equal to two yen during this period. Skirting the issue of the significance of the large per capita differences hidden by these totals, it is enough for the present discussion to point out that until nearly the end of the century the absolute amount of capital goods imported was a secondary consideration in accounting for the difference between Chinese and Japanese experience.

In homely terms, the situation in China was one of having led the horse to water but being unable to make him drink it. Foreign commerce, as in the case of Japan, was a highway for the introduction of modern science, machine technology, and Western forms of business organization: In the treaty ports and foreign concessions enterprising Chinese merchants or officials would have had ample access to Western experience. In those exceptional cases when the horse did drink, he apparently did so in some style. A commercial mission of the Blackburn Chamber of Commerce which toured China in 1896-1897 reported that the equipment of the few Chinese-owned cotton mills which they had visited was "as complete in every respect as the most modern of our English factories, and no expense has been spared in buying machinery and appliances of the latest and most approved designs." The Chinese were producing iron and steel at Hanyang with modern equipment purchased in Europe by Chang Chih-tung two years before the Japanese government began its iron and steel works at Yawata in 1896—a fact about which Chang and Sheng Hsuan-huai were not slow to boast. These instances are evidence at least of the accessibility of modern technology, but there were few takers.

Nor does it appear that the privileged status of foreigners and the treaty tariff were differentiating factors of any importance, for these were not abrogated in Japan until 1899. And although the trend was toward eliminating or reducing the role of the foreigner, it has been estimated that even in 1887 nearly 90 per cent of Japanese foreign trade was handled by foreign merchants. This proportion fell to 80 per cent in 1890, but was still more than 60 per cent in 1900. While corresponding figures for late nineteenth-century China would show the foreigner in a larger and undiminishing role, before 1895 the difference was not yet so prominent.

The essential qualitative distinction between the effects of foreign commerce on China and Japan was, as Lockwood has put it, that Japanese foreign trade was an "activator of change." That is, in addition to providing the means for the importation of technology from the advanced industrial nations, it supplied a motive or an impulse for new investment of the modern type. The development of the foreign market for Japanese exports hastened the growth of industry by making possible large-scale production and its attendant economies even with an initially limited domestic market. Why was this possible for Japan and not for China? For an explanation we turn again to the shadowy but crucial question of motivation, and then to the myth of the unlimited Chinese market.

Japanese aggressiveness and resourcefulness in foreign trade and the active part played by the Japanese government are described by Englishmen from Lancashire who were in China in 1896:

> This conduct in business is well illustrated by Japan's action in regard to Shashih [Shasi], a Yangtsze city, made a Treaty Port by the Shimonoseki Treaty. Here the Japanese have secured premises which have already been converted into a Trade Museum, where are shown articles suitable to Chinese wants, particularly textiles. To all samples are attached full particulars, and on these the persons in attendance are prepared to quote the book orders. The Museum is under the auspices of the Japanese Government, and is directly controlled by their Consul, already established in buildings acquired for the purposes of a Consulate.
>
> In strong contrast to this is the fact that at this time an English Consul had been assigned to the port, but had not taken up residence there, our "Consulate" being a large Chinese house boat, moored to the city shore of the river!

These are manifestations of the forces of modernization and growth set in motion after the Meiji Restoration. Foreign commerce could function as an "activator of change" only within a situation in which the government and mercantile classes were prepared to utilize it actively for certain generally accepted national goals. If, as in the case of China, international trade was largely a means wherewith the powers were acting upon China rather than a conscious instrument in the hands of an "enlightened" ruling class, it could not contribute greatly to modernization. These remarks have particular reference to the period before 1899 when both China and Japan were still burdened with a conventional five per cent tariff imposed by international treaty, and may be illustrated by the fate of traditional-type exports in the two countries.

Although by 1900 cotton yarn and piece goods and silk fabric accounted for 22 per cent of Japanese exports, indicating that industrialization was beginning to make considerable headway, down to the end of the century traditional-type exports occupied the first place in Japan as well as in China. For China exports of tea and silk were 92 per cent of the total in 1871, dropped to about 80 per cent during the 1880's, and were approximately 50 per cent in 1898. In Japan raw silk was responsible for roughly two thirds of the total exports in the period 1868-1893. Even in 1908 raw-silk exports were nearly double the value of manufactured cotton and silk exports. Raw silk then was a key commodity, the sale of which abroad provided a large portion of the foreign exchange in China and Japan. But Japan was rapidly gaining on China as a supplier of silk: In 1905 each provided one third of the world's supply; by 1913 Japan was well ahead, with 44.3 per cent to China's 31.1 per cent. China lost her leading position as a supplier of silk because of the elephantine conservatism of her traditional peasant producers and merchanting bodies. International trade demanded a better product and a standardized one, which could be achieved only if large-scale centralized organization were introduced from outside the peasant economy to superintend cocoon production and silk reeling. In Japan this organization was provided by the government and the large mercantile houses, such as the Mitsui Bussan Kaisha, through the licensing of egg suppliers, improvement of the methods of the silk raisers, operation of modern filatures, and large-scale marketing of the silk. But in China there was neither a government actively concerned with promoting modernization of the economy nor merchants willing or capable of revolutionizing production and marketing practices. There was little of that intense activity which we have noted of the Japanese in Shasi, apparently little motivation to cope with the challenge of Japanese competition.

Aggravating the inadequacies of the Chinese themselves was the greater political and economic pressure of the foreign powers on China than on Japan. This, I submit, was in large part a function of the myth of the Chinese market. Japan's economic development owed a great debt to the existence of opportunities for the profitable export of Japanese manufactured goods. The principal markets for these were in China and southeast Asia. China, however, would have to depend entirely on the demand of its domestic market to take up the products of its infant industries. But the foreign powers, including Japan, were themselves very much concerned about the potentialities of the Chinese home market. This is a theme extending back to Lord Macartney's embassy of 1793 and continuing through the nineteenth century down to the present time. The lure of "400 million customers" was a potent one, however illusory it might have been in fact. Perhaps a factor contributing to Japan's ability to free herself from the unequal treaties and protect her sovereignty and economy from foreign incursions was the relative neglect by the European powers of what seemed a small prize beside the imagined fruits of the China trade. As late as 1897, these were described in such glowing terms as the following:

> China's trade possibilities are immeasurable. The sparing use and non-presence of foreign commodities are warrant enough of future expansion if a policy could be adopted which shall open up the entire country to the advantages of unrestricted commercial intercourse. . . .

Strenuous foreign efforts to promote the sale of their manufactures in the interior of China, combined with the right to undertake manufacturing in the treaty ports—employing relatively cheap Chinese labor and without the expense of transporting goods from Europe or Japan—made deep inroads into the limited Chinese domestic market. The gap left by the breakdown of handicraft production, which should have been the basis for the growth of China's own infant industries, in large measure was filled with the products of European factories.

Thus China's political and psychological inability to adapt her traditional peasant economy to the demands of international trade was coupled with economic pressure from the European powers to reduce greatly the positive effect that commerce had in China as compared with the case of Japan.

It was out of these conditions that the system of official supervision and merchant management developed. The economic outlook of his contemporaries, the fiscal weakness of the Peking government, and the structure of Chinese trade and commerce constituted the environment within which Sheng Hsuan-huai, the leading promoter of *kuan-tu shang-pan* industry, operated. Together with the facts of Sheng's personal life and public career, which will now be examined, these factors helped determine the form of organization and the manner of operation of the enterprises to be discussed in the succeeding chapters.

9

THE KUOMINTANG AND ECONOMIC STAGNATION, 1928=1937

Douglas S. Paauw

An assault upon the massive problem of economic stagnation fundamentally requires the pursuit of three kinds of basic social and economic changes. First, and perhaps most important, a society must either mobilize domestic savings or attract foreign financing in order to raise substantially its level of investment. This is the problem of financing. Second, these resources must be employed to change production functions in important sectors of the economy to provide increased yields from the utilization of the country's economic endowments. This is the problem of technology. Third, the society must revamp its institutions in such fashion that high levels of savings and investment are perpetuated and the search for new and more productive techniques of production—innovation—becomes a basic social propensity. This is the problem of institutional change.

Where economic stagnation has been the normal state of affairs for decades—or even centuries—as in China, these changes cannot ordinarily be induced without continued and determined prodding by the groups who hold political power. A judgment on stagnation or progress during a given period of Chinese economic history must be based, therefore, upon an evaluation of the nature of the economic program of empowered elite groups. The most tragic evi-

Dr. Paauw is Director, Center for Development Planning, National Planning Association. In recent years he has concentrated on the study of problems of economic development in Southeast Asia. He is the author of *Financing Economic Development: The Indonesian Case,* Free Press and Center for International Studies, Massachusetts Institute of Technology, 1960. The present article is reprinted, with permission, from *The Journal of Asian Studies,* Vol. 16, No. 2 (February 1957), 213-220. Copyright © 1957 by The Association for Asian Studies, Inc.

dence of economic stagnation lies in the performance of men who have both an awareness of the problem of economic stagnation and the power to attack it but whose outlooks, objectives, and motivations lead them elsewhere.

Whatever indictments can be made against Kuomintang economic performance during the Nanking period, it is neither fair nor accurate to maintain that this was a period of complete failure and retrogression. The Kuomintang itself publicized many of its positive economic accomplishments, which are, in fact, a matter of record. These advances, however, failed to counteract long historical trends toward stagnating or falling per capita incomes.

In many ways we witnessed a start on the long road to establishing preconditions toward the three fundamental changes which lead to economic progress. In the financial field, the currency system was unified and a modern paper money system was eventually adopted. The confusion of the old currency system based on a variable unit, the tael, was virtually ended. The government set about to reform its fiscal system by centralizing its pattern of indirect taxation, demanding control of China's tariff policy, and experimenting with annual budgets. In the field of technological change, the Kuomintang sought and received technical advice from the League of Nations. Notable progress was made in transportation and communications—much of this late in the Nanking period under the inspiration of an able and aggressive Minister of Communications. The government emphasized development of the power industry, and capacity was significantly expanded. In the area of social and institutional change, however, the Kuomintang attempted to remold from the fragments of revolution and decay a Confucian society with a narrow and powerful apex. Social and economic power, therefore, tended to follow its traditional orbit, severely limiting the extent to which the public could contribute to economic progress.

This unique Kuomintang formula for emphasizing some aspects of the technical preconditions for economic growth while suppressing institutional change, as we might expect, did not lead to significant progress. The record shows little more than the continuance of economic stagnation during the Nanking period. While conclusive studies of the behavior of output and investment have not yet been written, we do have access to studies which support this conclusion. The persistence of stagnant levels of agricultural output is documented by Liu Ta-chung's national income estimate.

Working from annual data collected by the National Agricultural Research Bureau, Liu's results show that total agricultural output increased by less than one per cent in the five-year period 1932-36. (1931, the first year covered by Liu's study, is unsatisfactory for our purpose because a general flood severely disrupted agricultural production in that year.) Stagnation is even more apparent from the behavior of the gross national product in these years. According to Liu, total output in 1936 was approximately the same as in 1932 for the 22 provinces, and average output for the 1932-36 period was somewhat lower than the 1932 figure. On the other hand, there is evidence which suggests that population was expanding by at least one half of one per cent per year. These data indicate, therefore, that the growth of total output failed to keep pace with the increase in China's population over five years of the decade of Kuomintang rule from Nanking.

Liu reported nonagricultural output in 1936 at five per cent above the 1931 level, although output from some sectors showed considerable growth while others declined. He believes that output from modern manufacturing industries as a whole showed steady growth. However, Liu obtained these results by making the rather dubious assumption that there was a one to one correlation between employment and output. An actual index of production for seven leading modern industries, constructed by the Central Bank of China, shows no increase in output over a 3½ year period (1932-35).

Economic stagnation is also apparent from the investment record of these years. After considerable revision and extension of his earlier work, Ou Pao-san presented his final estimates for China's investment performance (1931-36) in his Harvard doctoral thesis (1949). For these years, Ou's study reveals that domestic investment was inadequate to provide for maintenance of China's capital stock by replacement. Disinvestment totaled over 1¾ billion yuan in the period 1931-36. This process of capital erosion was scarcely reversed by net foreign borrowing which allowed the economy just about to maintain its capital facilities at existing levels.

Ou's results make Chinese investment performance look better than it actually was. Virtually all of the new foreign investment reported took place in Manchuria, which was included in Ou's study. If China proper, the actual locus of Kuomintang authority, were considered as a unit, Ou's results would clearly suggest a trend toward depletion of China's capital stock during the Nanking government period. This conclusion is confirmed by a recent study which suggests that the total value of foreign investment in China proper actually fell between 1931 and 1936.

The Kuomintang and the government it maintained in power were formally committed to programs of economic reform and development to improve the people's livelihood. Yet economic stagnation continued during the Nanking government period, and the average level of consumption appears to have fallen. The reasons behind this discrepancy between avowed intent and result require elaboration.

It is important to observe, first of all, that economic reform and development were not in fact given high priority on the programming level, carrying significant claims upon the resources at the disposal of the government. Instead, the Kuomintang sought to achieve popular support and unification by military force and political maneuvering. Even before 1928, the ruling groups in the Kuomintang began to back away from acting upon their formal commitment to the kind of social revolution which Sun Yat-sen had envisaged. Throughout the Nanking period, Chiang Kai-shek's policies gave the highest and almost exclusive priority to unification by force, which was pressed to the limit of the regime's meager resources. The reality of this commitment is reflected in the government's expenditure pattern during the decade 1928-37. Expenditures for defense absorbed about one half of the government's annual budgets, while funds allocated and spent for economic development and reform were virtually nil. In spite of the Kuomintang's preoccupation with unification by force, however, the Nanking government held secure and complete political control in only two provinces in 1937.

One of the most illuminating aspects of the discrepancy between what the Kuomintang preached and what it practiced is found in the government's adaptation of Sun Yat-sen's economic principles to ends which would have repulsed Sun. As early as the First Party Congress in 1924, the paraphernalia of Sun's programs for economic reconstruction were adopted as official Kuomintang policy. Adherence to these programs was stubbornly reiterated throughout the two decades of Kuomintang authority on the mainland. But performance was quite another question, and in its distortion of Sunist principles in the Nanking period, the Kuomintang defined a course not only contributing to economic stagnation but perhaps sowing the seeds for its political debacle many years later.

Sun Yat-sen's principle of "people's livelihood" was formally interpreted by the Kuomintang to embody two major guides to the formulation of economic policy—"equalization of land use" and "regulation of capital." Equalization of land use involved the eventual goal of ownership of land by cultivators to protect the peasantry from the growing power of the landlord class. Regulation of capital sought to assure the protection of the various economic classes through government guidance and control of investment in large-scale enterprise, both through state ownership and progressive taxation. By the time the Kuomintang came to power, top government elite groups had lost interest in pressing for the agrarian revolution to which they were pledged. Land Laws, patterned after Sun's model, were enacted in 1930 and later years, but there was no effort to enforce them. Fundamentally, this reflected a basic Kuomintang propensity to base its government upon the urban sector of the economy, or more precisely, upon the industrial base in a few relatively advanced provinces where control extended from top to bottom.

The Nanking government's performance on the other tenet of people's livelihood, regulation of capital, began the fateful march to bureaucratic capitalism, which eventually cost the regime whatever ideals it had about social welfare. Interpreting this principle to its own satisfaction, the economic elite set out to achieve control over the economy's strategic industries—banking, mining, power, for example. The economic literature of the Nanking period, much of it written by the government elite, is replete with justifications for this version of "the controlled economy" (*t'ung-chih ching-chi*). Through a variety of screened maneuvers, however, industries which the government had transferred to its ownership, began to gravitate into the private control of important members of the Kuomintang elite. Under the guise of Sun's principle, a small but powerful group of government officials came to dominate much of China's modern industry and banking resources as private business magnates. Sun Yat-sen had envisaged regulation of private enterprise to insure social welfare, but this trend placed large accumulations of wealth beyond government control through a distortion of Sun's own principle.

The China Development Finance Corporation, a banking syndicate organized in 1934 to purchase and expand existing industrial enterprises, was one of the most notorious avenues to bureaucratic capitalism. Sponsored by the government and under the firm control of its chairman, who incidentally held high government positions related to the economic field, this Corporation had managed to take over several strategic industries from the National Reconstruction Commission by 1937. Eventually these industries fell under the control of a few government officials who had been active in promoting the parent organization.

Lacking a systematic approach to the problem of stagnation, the Nanking government's impact upon economic growth lay mainly in its relationship to the conditions for development in the private sector. The trend toward bureaucratic capitalism was important in this respect, but its effects were aggravated by the regime's other economic policies. Fiscal and financial policies were emphasized by the Nanking government; and, focused as they were upon the modern sector of the economy, had considerable significance for its prospects for growth.

One of the major shortcomings of the Nanking regime was its inability to finance a level of expenditures adequate to accomplish either unification or reconstruction. Government expenditures averaged about 3½ per cent of the gross national product, and tax revenues were considerably less. Despite much ado about fiscal reform in the early Nanking period, the government was unable to channel a significant share of total national income through the public finances. Behind this failure lay the 1928 decision to abstain from taxation of the rural sector, and the government's inability or unwillingness to levy progressive income taxation upon upper incomes throughout the society generally. About 85 per cent of total tax revenues were raised from indirect taxes on foreign trade and commodities of industrial origin, the remainder by a number of other indirect levies. The value of output taxed by the central government did not represent more than 10 or 15 per cent of the national income, located in a relatively small geographical area.

Tax revisions during the Nanking period did not involve structural changes in the tax system, designed to spread the tax burden more equitably or generally. Instead, the pattern of indirect taxation which the Nanking government inherited from its predecessor was preserved and more sharply focused upon the modern sector of the economy. Tax reforms, to which the Kuomintang pointed with pride, were essentially devices to promote central control of existing taxes in the coastal provinces, and to increase their yield by imposing higher rates.

Although not employing fiscal resources to finance economic development, the government felt it necessary to prosecute a level of expenditures which greatly exceeded tax revenues. During the Nanking period, an average of 25 per cent of government expenditures were financed by borrowing. Borrowing domestically, the government promoted a relationship between itself and the banking system which tended to stifle economic growth in the private sector. It succeeded in molding China's modern banking system into a highly centralized structure, dominated by four government banks. By the end of 1935, the government banks themselves held 40 per cent of the total capital and reserves, and 56 per cent of total deposits of all modern banks. The government also held four fifths of the shares of private modern banks owning 61 per cent of the combined resources of all private banks.

Having achieved dominant control of China's modern banking resources, the government did not wield its power for purposes of economic development. Rather than drawing upon the central banking group for cheap credit, the Nanking government chose to turn to the modern banking community generally for high-cost credit. Government bonds were sold to the banking system at sharp discounts from their face value, placing the effective interest rates anywhere from 20 to 40 per cent of the proceeds. These bonds were highly remunerative to lenders, since they were used to secure note issue during much of the period, and because they became the prime form of speculative activities. Government borrowing, therefore, directly diverted savings from the private sector by channeling them to the finance of current government operations, and indirectly by tying up liquid funds in speculation on the government bond market. One Chinese writer estimated that 50 per cent of Shanghai's total liquid assets were invested in government bonds, and that much of the remainder was diverted to speculation in these same credit instruments. Nanking government finance, therefore, promoted the diversion of the economy's stocks of savings from investment to speculative uses. In addition, it raised the cost of bank credit to the point where private entrepreneurs could not make use of bank credit for productive purposes. Accordingly, there was a definite shift in the loan portfolios of modern banks from commercial and industrial credit to government bonds. The reasons behind this whole course of events no doubt lie in the fact that each of the four government banks, with extensive control in the private banking system, was personally dominated by individuals who exercised both government authority and capitalistic power in the private sector of the economy.

The impact of this unwholesome system of political economy upon economic growth will be analyzed here only in terms of its effect upon savings and investment. It is instructive to observe, first, that the government made little direct contribution to the level of investment through its own expenditure pattern, and that no net savings were realized on government account for any year in the Nanking period. The government's impact upon these variables, therefore, lay almost exclusively in its relationship to private capital formation.

In limiting its fiscal impact to the modern sector of the economy, the Nanking government placed itself in a position from which it could not promote mobilization of financial resources from the rural sector to finance government operations or developmental investment. It was similarly impotent to employ fiscal measures to induce productive use of upper incomes earned in this sector. Unequal income distribution perpetuated a group of high-income recipients who employed their earnings to finance high standards of consumption as well as to maintain their position through land purchase and speculative marketing and credit operations. Nanking fiscal policy failed to halt this diversion of potential savings to nonproductive outlets.

Tax policies in the modern sector were designed to produce maximum yields from the existing pattern of regressive taxation. The Kuomintang failed to consider the economic effects of its tax burden, or partially to shift this burden to upper income groups. Customs duties, providing for both import and export taxation, fell largely upon lower income groups or producers, and were not protective in nature. They failed to provide incentives to investment in China's leading modern industry, cotton textiles, for example, since imported raw materials and other producers' goods were taxed at rates almost as high as the duty on imported textiles. Export duties were collected throughout the period, even though foreign demand for China's product was weak and elastic. In both cases, therefore, customs taxation tended to affect investment decisions adversely.

Taxation of industrially produced commodities clearly discriminated against the domestic Chinese producer. Taxes were assessed against these commodities under a schedule which imposed higher rates on low-quality products than on superior qualities. Reflecting the shortage of Chinese capital and inferior levels of technology, Chinese firms tended to specialize in the production of low-quality goods, while higher qualities were either produced in foreign-owned firms or imported. Oriented toward lower-income groups, Chinese producers disposed of their output in markets in which demand was highly elastic in terms of prices. Since these taxes were shifted forward to the consumer, they severely limited demand, reducing the profitability of Chinese industrial production and limiting opportunities for expanding the scale of production. Foreign producers, on the other hand, operated in higher-quality markets where the price elasticity of demand was considerably less and where commodity taxes were a lower percentage of the total market price.

Equally critical, however, Nanking taxation tended to affect the broad range of profit-making opportunities in favor of enterprise with little relation to economic growth. Virtually no central taxes were levied on profits from commercial and speculative activities which continued to yield high profits from short-term commitments of funds. By failing to impose a tax burden on these activities, the Kuomintang government overlooked an important source of revenue, violated the ability-to-pay principle of taxation, and neglected to employ its fiscal power to increase the attractiveness of output-increasing investment.

While discouraging the expansion of Chinese investment in production, Kuomintang policies also tended to limit the availability of savings for this purpose. Although the society's saving potential was increased by a growing inequality of income distribution, and deposits in the modern banking system actually increased, these accumulations were not made available for financing developmental investment. The government itself encouraged the diversion of these funds to the finance of current governmental expenditures and speculative uses in Shanghai and other financial centers. It is also significant to note that the Chinese banking system was unable to engage in net credit creation during the Nanking period, failing to provide the leverage that has been so important to financing economic development in the West. Although the Kuomintang held extensive financial control over China's credit system, it failed to support the money market with facilities to convert longer-term loans into liquid assets should the necessity arise. Since the Central Bank provided no rediscount or other emergency credit facilities, Chinese modern banks restricted their credit to short-term, highly liquid or well-secured qualities. The banking system, by and large, failed to channel the savings it actually mobilized to investment uses, and was unable to add to its supply of financial resources by forcing savings upon the community.

This analysis suggests that the Kuomintang was not prepared on either the conceptual or policy level to cope with the problem of economic stagnation. The powers of government were not used to provide financing of economic development, to induce technological change, or to encourage institutional reform. Worse than this, Nanking government policies fostered traditional uses of the economy's resources and output in patterns which aggravated the dynamics of stagnation. Income distribution became more unequal; potential savings were diverted to hoarding and speculation; investment in improved technology was discouraged. The trend toward bureaucratic capitalism, a historical model of government relationship to business with much precedent in China, flourished under the blessing of Sun Yat-sen's name and party resolutions. Its objective was control by the few rather than the expansion of output. The regime's fiscal and monetary policies, and even its lack of concern with the agrarian sector of the economy, reflected this underlying propensity.

These were not preconditions for economic growth. The government had less capacity to promote economic development in 1937 than a decade earlier. In the private sector, the climate for growth was less favorable than it had been when the Chinese nemesis, imperialism, had held rule. Foreign investment in China proper was less significant than it had been during the preceding fifty years. Its withdrawal was not matched by increased domestic investment. Encumbered with the economic values and policies which we have described, it is doubtful that the Kuomintang could have solved China's traditional problem of economic stagnation with more political control and less Japanese aggression.

10

SOME REFLECTIONS ON CHINESE COMMUNIST ECONOMIC POLICY

Peter Schran

PROBLEMS OF STRATEGY AND TACTICS

To cope with the aftermath of war and with problems of under-development, the Chinese Communists could count on their own capabilities, on the "advanced experiences of the Soviet Union," and—hopefully—on "600 million people" with their traditional tools, but on few things else. Arable land was rather scarce and could not be increased to a large extent. Even after its rehabilitation, industrial plant and equipment did not amount to much. Its most important component, the Manchurian industrial complex of Japanese origin, had been damaged severely by Soviet dismantling and had to be repaired at great cost by means of "redemption." Modern industry was concentrated in the coastal areas. Modern means of transportation and communication did not extend very far. The amounts of material aid given by the Soviet Union, important as they were, were relatively small, and no aid was forthcoming from other parts of the world.

Moreover, even the major assets on which the Chinese Communists could draw were of inferior quality. The "advanced experiences of the Soviet Union" had to be adapted to Chinese reality. Because of limited economic development in the past and due to their own limited opportunities and experiences during the preceding years, they themselves lacked the technical and administra-

Dr. Schran, Assistant Professor of Economics, Yale University, has just completed a study of the structure of income in Communist China. This article is reprinted, with permission, from *The China Quarterly*, No. 11 (July-September 1962), 58-77. Copyright © 1962 by The Congress for Cultural Freedom. Minor deletions have been made in the article.

tive competence to utilize their political power fully at once. The vast majority of their "600 million people" did not qualify any better for the tasks ahead, for the same reasons. Indeed, most of them possessed little more than physical energy, the few skills necessary to handle primitive tools, and—hopefully in many cases—keen minds. Finally, past events had left the economy in a state of severe fragmentation, and common lofty sentiments could not be expected to prevail for long over diverse economic interests.

While the Chinese Communists had to rely chiefly on themselves and on their abundant labour force in their attempt to advance China economically, they could depend on Marxist-Leninist doctrine for an outline of the general course of action that they would have to follow in pursuit of their goal. Economic growth required increasing accumulation, increasing work efforts, and increasing learning efforts. Doctrine asserted that such increases could be induced by changes in the distributive system to "distribution according to labour" and added that changes in the distributive system were dependent on changes in its determinant, the distribution of ownership of the means of production. By abolishing private ownership of the means of production, private nonlabour income and with it "parasitic" consumption would be eliminated. Consequently "surplus value" could be accumulated *in toto,* and labour efforts would increase, since everyone would depend for his livelihood on his labour income. By paying everyone according to the type, amount, and quality of his work, furthermore, still greater work efforts and learning efforts would be encouraged. Thus, transition to the Socialist mode of production would be conducive to economic growth.

Although the Chinese Communists had the design for a suitable system of social relations, some not-so-advanced experiences of the Soviet Union, as well as some lessons which they had learned by themselves, warned them to be careful in their endeavor to reconstruct society according to this blueprint. They were well aware of the problem that "social consciousness" need not change at once or—in specific instances—even at all with changes in the mode of production, and that a rapid transition to socialism might provoke "negative" rather than "positive" reactions, with obvious consequences for the state of the economy. They saw still more clearly that the state of the arts could not be changed entirely in the short run, since the ability to communicate modern production techniques as well as the ability to adapt to them were limited. Indeed, both changes seemed to require longer periods of habituation, enhanced by indoctrination and training. Therefore, a process of gradual advance on the "road toward Socialism" seemed to be called for.

Since technical and social constraints limited the extent to which labor force and means of production could be increased and improved, the Chinese Communists had to solve an intricate factor-allocation problem in the interest of increasing the rate of growth as much as possible over a short period of time. On the one hand, current resources had to be devoted to the task of removing or diminishing current technical and social constraints, because any advance in this direction would set free additional human energy and additional means of production for future use in production. On the other hand, current resources had to be allocated to current production in such a fashion that it, too, would contribute as many resources as possible to future production.

The solution to the problem reflected the influence of Marxist-Leninist doctrine, Soviet experience, and Maoist understanding of the initial conditions. It stressed besides indoctrination and training the development of producer-goods industries relative to consumer-goods industries, the development of industry relative to handicrafts and agriculture, and generally the development of modern economic activities relative to traditional economic activities on a pattern which subsequently came to be known as "walking on two legs." The modern sector of the economy was made to grow by "Western methods," while the traditional sector of the economy was encouraged to advance by "indigenous methods."

DEVELOPMENT OF MODERN INDUSTRY, 1949-57

The scarcest and potentially most productive factors, modern means of production and highly trained labor, were concentrated on modern industry and on heavy industry in particular. Every effort was made to increase their numbers and their productivity by importing equipment and advisers, by training and indoctrinating the labour force, and by changing the distributive system. Interindustry wage differentials served to attract labourers to heavy industry, labor grade differentials encouraged them to "study," bonuses and piece rates induced them to exert more effort, and frontier allowances made life in remote areas less undesirable.

The national bourgeoisie—that is, the relatively thin stratum of entrepreneurs, capitalists, and managers in private industry and commerce—were subjected to the policy of "utilizing, restricting, and reconstructing." Since the Chinese Communists had to rely on their services especially in light industry and in general during the initial period of rehabilitation, their expropriation was postponed in most instances until it appeared to be "both necessary and feasible" in the context of planned marketing and planned production. Following advances in the government's ability to control the private sector, capitalists were limited instead increasingly in their rights to their property and to the profits which they made. It did not take long until accumulation in one form or the other claimed the greatest portion of private profits, with the consequence that dividend payments decreased severely, so that capitalists had to depend for their livelihood primarily on their managerial salaries or on other labor income. In 1956, finally, capitalists were exposed to the prospect of total proletarization when the government "redeemed" their productive property with the promise to pay fixed interest (five per cent) on the value of their reassessed net assets for a limited period (seven years).

However much specific official claims may be distrusted, there remains little doubt that the efforts to develop the modern sector rapidly yielded impressive results. With speedy increases in the "quantity and quality" of both labor and means of production, industry's productive capacity expanded at rapid rates. Moreover, whenever industry did not depend significantly on supplies from extrasectoral sources or whenever it received such supplies in sufficient quantities, its output grew similarly rapidly. Thus, heavy industrial production mushroomed in particular since heavy industry was favoured by the massive allocation of trained labor and modern equipment, since it utilized primarily nonagricultural raw materials, and since its demands on other sectors were met with priority. Light industry, however, did not benefit from any of these advantages to a similar extent. Besides being relegated to second place in the allocation of especially scarce factors of production, it depended heavily on agricultural raw materials. Therefore, in distinction to its capacity, the output of light industry changed generally in accordance with changes in the sales volume of crops destined for industrial processing and thus was determined by the Chinese Communists' success or failure in developing agriculture by means of social reforms and improvements in "indigenous methods."

DEVELOPMENT OF AGRICULTURE, 1949-57

Increases in the imports and in the domestic production of modern agricultural production materials, implements, and machinery as well as the construction of major dams and power networks indicate that agriculture was not deprived entirely of modern means of production. Yet it is also evident that the impact of all of these improvements was not so great as to change the nature of the factors and factor combinations basically in the short run. For the time being, the mass of the peasants continued to till the land during short seasons according to time-honoured principles with the few, primitive tools that had also withstood the dust of ages. Since they produced most of these tools themselves and processed much of their agricultural produce for their own consumption domestically, they remained highly self-sufficient as well.

Under the constraint that the growth of modern industry was not to be sacrificed for the development of agriculture, the Chinese Communists could attempt to increase agricultural output by increasing the input of traditional factors of production as much as possible and by improving them and their combinations as much as possible without withdrawing additional inputs from industry. Furthermore, they could attempt to improve the degree of utilization of agricultural output by eliminating peasant processing of agricultural products in favour of industrial processing. Again, training, indoctrination, and changes in the distributive system recommended themselves to the Chinese Communists as proper stimulants. Besides being good politics at the moment, the initial land reform served several economic ends. It eliminated practically all land rents and thus made everyone dependent on labor income, thereby increasing the rural labor force. It also eliminated landlord consumption out of land rents and consequently enabled the government to increase not only peasant consumption but also public accumulation by means of increased rural taxation. Mutual aid teams served to acquaint the peasants with the advantages of group work on a larger than familial scale and helped to induce them to invest in implements which they could not afford individually. Agricultural production co-operatives aimed at increasing the area of cultivated land and at improving its cultivation by means of merging and reclaiming land, by improving the soil and increasing the extent of irrigation, and so forth. This kind of "primitive accumulation" required of the peasants that they increase their contributions of work efforts to agriculture considerably and especially during the lengthy off-seasons. In the interest of promoting urban-rural division of labor, planned purchasing had limited the peasants already in subsidiary work activities which competed with industrial activities. Now this measure was reinforced by collective marketing of collective produce and supplemented by limitations to the land and livestock that could be cared for on a familial scale. In order to provide positive inducements as well, collective income was distributed increasingly "according to labor." By means of co-operative accumulation funds, rural accumulation and rural investment in modern means of production were advanced to some extent.

While official claims concerning achievements in agriculture are particularly dubious, it may well be said that in comparison with industry, agriculture developed little at best. Since most traditional inputs—notably the number of peasant work days—seem to have increased over time, and since various improvements in the factors and methods of production seem to have been instituted with reasonable success on a relatively large scale, there appears to be little reason for challenging the assertion that agricultural output did increase. Yet, any statement concerning the degree of advance is complicated by such imponderables as the quality of collective management, changes in peasant motivation due to collectivization, and natural fortunes. Generally, it seems safe to conclude that natural conditions were not particularly favorable to agriculture during most of the period and that, on balance, collectivization benefited the growing of crops which did not require intensive individual attention while it harmed animal husbandry and truck gardening, which depended on such care.

Even if the official claims are accepted at face value, however, they show that on the average, agricultural output did not grow as fast as light industrial capacity, and that the adequate utilization of the latter required decreases in the *share* of agricultural output which was retained by the peasants for their own consumption. While such decreases were also desirable in view of the advantages of division of labor between agriculture and industry, they were subject to a number of constraints. Bottlenecks in transportation as well as other technical and social considerations prevented the elimination of rural processing of food crops for peasant consumption. Greatly increased labor efforts in agriculture necessitated at least some im-

provements in peasant diets. And food requirements in general
limited the extent to which technical crops could be grown. Thus,
although sales of agricultural products seem to have increased twice
as fast as agricultural output, limited agricultural growth continued
to restrain light industry in the attempt to increase the output of
various consumer goods.

DISTRIBUTION PROBLEMS, 1949-57

By approaching problems of economic growth within the confines
of an exceedingly narrow time horizon and by favoring the development of producer-goods industries relative to that of consumer-
goods industries and to that of agriculture, the Chinese Communists
necessarily burdened themselves with a troublesome intersectoral
distribution problem. "Distribution according to labour" implied
that, in all sectors of production, increments in labor income depended largely on increments in the amount and quality of work
undertaken. Since the latter tended to be measured in terms of work
results—that is, increments in output—income per laborer increased
with increases in output. Because the initial capital stock as well as
its increments were invested primarily in modern industry and especially in heavy industry, output per laborer and with it income
per laborer grew much more rapidly in heavy industry than in light
industry, much more rapidly in the modern sector than in the
traditional sector, and least in agriculture.

While the Chinese Communists considered it necessary to estab-
lish wage differentials in favor of the priority sectors, they did not
deem it desirable to increase intersectoral earnings differentials
continuously. On the contrary, they realized that the limited increases in consumer goods, and especially in consumer goods with
agricultural raw material content, depended largely on the increased
labor efforts of the peasants. Peasant awareness of an increasingly
disadvantageous earnings position, however, could lead to dissatisfaction which might manifest itself in decreasing work efforts,
evasion of delivery norms, and "blind flight to the cities." Since the
increases in consumer-goods output, limited as they were, were
important because they provided the means to pay for additional
imports of means of production which were required by the priority
sectors, and because they made it possible to stimulate further increases in labor efforts through added "material incentives," the

Chinese Communists decided to compensate agriculture to some extent for the productivity gains which it had to forgo.

In an effort to further their control over markets and prices for agricultural consumer goods at the same time, they chose to subsidize the peasants by manipulating the urban-rural terms of trade in their favor. The purchase prices for compulsory deliveries of agricultural products increased significantly, while the rural retail prices of industrial products remained fairly stable. As a consequence of this measure, the peasants were left with amounts of agricultural produce for their own consumption which apparently increased at least slightly, and with increasing amounts of cash in exchange for increasing amounts of compulsory deliveries which were bought by the state at increasing prices. Cash income, in turn, could be spent primarily on various industrial products with little agricultural raw material content. The most needed item, cotton cloth, was in short supply and therefore rationed.

Since the Chinese Communists seem to have considered it politically advisable to maintain a fair degree of price stability, they made every effort to diminish the impact of increases in the purchase prices for agricultural products on the urban cost of living. Retail prices for unprocessed agricultural products seem to have increased less due to reductions in the cost (and quality) of distribution during the course of socialization of private commerce. Productivity gains in light industry seem to have compensated for increased raw material cost. And the prices of various consumer goods with little or no agricultural raw material content seem to have decreased correspondingly. As a consequence of these measures, increases in the urban cost of living seem to have been small. Yet, since increases in the output and in the compulsory purchases of agricultural staples were not very large, and since a portion of the limited increment had to be exported, supplies of basic necessities fell short of demand at most times, and practically all basic foods as well as cotton cloth had to be subject to rationing. Thus, the urban population, too, seems to have been left with amounts of daily necessities which increased slightly over time, and with cash to spare for goods of nonagricultural origin.

THE GREAT LEAP FORWARD

Economic policy and the economy did not develop as smoothly during the initial period as the above account might suggest.

But there remains little doubt that the Chinese Communists succeeded surprisingly well in their attempts to induce rapid economic growth in such a form that it was compatible with minor "improvements in the people's level of living." Yet, if the initial policy measures produced such notable results, why did the Chinese Communists resort to "leaping forward," thus taking the risk of endangering future economic development as well as past "achievements"? This question can be answered in a speculative form on the basis of the preceding presentation.

Economic growth and the development of the modern sector in particular were restricted in various ways by the slow advance of the traditional sector and especially of agriculture. In order to accelerate the rate of growth of the modern sector and of the economy in general further, this restraining influence of limited agricultural development had to be overcome. Progress in this direction could be attempted through a variety of measures. If heavy industry had to rely largely on imported means of production, further increases in the rate of growth of heavy industrial output could be brought about by decreasing the degree of its dependence on these imports as well as by increasing the rate of growth of consumer-goods exports as the prerequisite to producer-goods imports. Increases in the degree of heavy industrial self-sufficiency depended on increased labor and learning efforts by the industrial labor force. Increases in the rate of growth of consumer-goods exports required corresponding increases in the rate of consumer-goods production or, at least, decreases in the rate of increase of domestic consumer-goods supplies and possibly even decreases in the amount of the latter. If both goals were to be pursued in the absence of disproportionately large increases in consumer-goods production, great increases in the efforts of the industrial labor force had to be brought about by small increases in consumer-goods supplies, or had to be induced in spite of decreases in the latter. Evidently, such an advance was impossible without corresponding "ideological progress" of the workers or of the peasants or of both, depending on the pattern of allocation of consumer-goods supplies.

The amount of modern consumer goods that could be produced was determined primarily by the amount of agricultural raw materials that could be supplied. Further increments could be achieved by decreases in light industry's dependence on agriculture as well as by changes in the agricultural sector. The former move required increased labor and learning efforts, as well as increased material investment in consumer-goods industries, and thus advances in the development of certain branches of heavy industry or increases in the imports of producer goods for light industry. Obviously, such measures could withdraw means of production from heavy industry in the short run, while they would yield significant results only in the long run. Increases in the amount of marketed agricultural products could result from increases in agricultural production as well as from decreases in the share of retained products. As a consequence of limited material investment, increases in agricultural output depended on disproportionately large increases in labor efforts as well as on fortuitous circumstances. In the absence of large increases in agricultural output, substantial increments in the marketed portion would be compatible at best with small increments and quite possibly only with decrements in the retained portion of agricultural output. Moreover, in the absence of significant advances toward industrial self-sufficiency, large increases in exports could lead to decreases in the rural supplies of industrial consumer goods. Thus, further increments in the rate of economic growth could require decreases in the amounts of agricultural products which could be retained by the peasantry, as well as decreases in the amount of industrial consumer goods which could be purchased by them. Quite clearly, then, further advances might not be possible without significant "ideological progress" of the peasantry as well.

In summary, accelerated economic growth could not be achieved without substantial increases in labor and learning efforts or without rapid increases in the rate of accumulation, but the extent to which "ideological incentives" had to replace "material incentives" depended largely on the rate at which output in the traditional sector, and especially in agriculture, could be made to grow. In the absence of large increases in the supply of modern means of production by industry, agricultural output could be increased by disproportionate increases in agricultural work efforts with given methods of production or by significant improvements in agricultural production techniques. Since the former change required correspondingly disproportionate advances in peasant "consciousness," improvements in the "indigenous methods" appeared as the *sine qua non* to accelerated growth.

The above deductions tend to explain the undertaking of the "great leap forward" and the institution of the commune system if they are based on a number of premises. On the one hand, the Chinese Communists must have been convinced that their past performance fell short of the best possible one, and that this shortcoming was attributable to their extreme caution. Such an opinion is indicated by concern about the fact that accumulation rates during the Chinese First Five-Year Plan Period had not reached the level of accumulation rates during the Soviet First Five-Year Plan Period, in combination with the recognition that the First Five-Year Plan had been overfulfilled even in agriculture and that the economy had been socialized with few complications. On the other hand, the Chinese Communists must have been aware of the danger that future growth of the traditional sector without improvements in the "indigenous methods" or without heavy investment was handicapped by the exhaustion of the excess supply of labor that had existed under the then current system of social organization in city and countryside. Most of the urban unemployed had been absorbed into industry or had been sent to the villages. Trades and handicrafts had been "rationalized" during the course of urban collectivization and socialization. Peasant workdays had been increased to the limit during the course of rural collectivization. In this situation, the "new agricultural methods" must have appeared as a *deus ex machina* for the reason that they made commune-ization—that is, the socialization of household activities—both "necessary" because females constituted the major labor reserve, and "possible" because experiments promised large gains from deep-ploughing, close planting, heavy fertilizing, and so forth.

At an earlier time, the Chinese Communists might have thought twice before starting a social transformation of such proportions and might have engaged in social experimentation over a longer period of time, since the prospects looked too bright to be true. In 1958, however, the tragedy took its course, probably because they were so convinced of their capabilities in consequence of previous successes which had exceeded their expectations. Socialization of household activities "freed" the women for agricultural production. Territorial organization facilitated developmental projects in the form of primitive accumulation, helped rural industrialization on a larger scale, and made it possible to eliminate "income disparities" between intelligentsia, workers, and peasants in the countryside, at the expense of the former two groups. On the presumption that "the law of diminishing returns had been disproved," planned output was to increase greatly. Everyone experimented with backyard furnaces for the opposite reason and in order to acquire technical know-how as well as in order to relieve modern industry of consumer-goods demands. For the latter purpose, too, many small establishments which made use of "primitive modern" methods developed everywhere and absorbed a large number of newly recruited laborers. Planned accumulation increased even more than planned output, and peasants were stimulated to fulfill and overfulfill these plans by means of systems of distribution which incorporated both the incentive elements, with respect to laboring and learning that industrial wage-grade systems provided, and Communist elements of "distribution according to need." During the autumn of 1958, "distribution according to need" became increasingly popular and spread even to the cities and to industry, where targets had been increased as well as reportedly fulfilled and overfulfilled to an unbelievable degree, where "work for the sake of working" had been advocated and practised to some extent, and where housewives had been "freed" for work in urban communes on a limited scale.

The results of this vast endeavor appear to have been truly impressive. People were induced to exhaust themselves totally in an attempt to "leap into Communism" and consequently created a mass of output, ranging from the most sophisticated machinery to brittle backyard iron. There is little doubt that agriculture prospered under the influences of favorable natural conditions and unprecedented work efforts and that per capita consumption of daily necessities increased due to it, if only for the reason that the increased work efforts had to be sustained. There are also indications that the momentum of the "leap" carried well into 1959, with similar results. But what happened once it became clear that nature could *not* be controlled and that the law of diminishing returns had *not* been disproved?

PROBLEMS OF CURRENT AND FUTURE DEVELOPMENT

Late in 1958, the Chinese Communists must have become aware of the fact that their hopes for disproportionate increases in agricultural output had been false. In consequence of this realization, they had to concern themselves with two problems:

In the short run, they had to worry about the cost of their misguided venture—that is, ultimately about disillusionment, lethargy and cynicism on the part of people who had exhausted themselves severely in pursuit of unattainable goals.

For the long run, they had to devise a new strategy of economic development which proceeded from the assumption that such goals were not attainable and which reconciled the desire for rapid economic growth with this constraint.

Common to both problems were thus the notions that agricultural growth could not be accelerated miraculously by "indigenous methods" and that control over the economy depended on the recognition of this fact. In various other respects, however, the problems differed considerably.

THE THREE HARD YEARS

During the early fifties, the Chinese Communists had cautioned repeatedly against instituting excessive targets for fear of negative repercussions. Once they had departed from this practice mistakenly in 1958 and 1959, they could predict for themselves the consequences with which they would have to deal. People had become frustrated to the extent that they not only accomplished less, but also simulated accomplishments in excess of the unreasonable demands that were made upon them. Thus not only production declined, but chaotic planning conditions developed as well, which brought about bad allocation of resources on a grand scale and consequently decreases in output beyond those resulting from decreased work efforts. Aggravated without doubt by continuously unfavorable natural conditions, these developments produced the "three hard years."

In order to cope with them, the Chinese Communists seem to have instituted a comprehensive program of rehabilitation under the slogan of "consolidating the gains" made during the first two years of the Second Five-Year Plan Period. Immediately after they had realized that the "new agricultural methods" would not produce staggering results, they relaxed agricultural production goals as well as accumulation targets, changed the system of communal distribution so that Communist elements decreased in importance and "distribution according to labor" became once again the guiding line, decentralized communal operations in agriculture, increased earnings differentials within the commune, and so forth. At the same time, they apparently attempted to make the best of some undoubted gains from "the great leap forward." The loss of "superstitions" and some newly acquired skills as well as increased material investment in agriculture facilitated improvements in traditional methods on a more modest scale. In addition, emphasis was placed on agricultural diversification as a safeguard against calamities.

In spite of all these measures, the Chinese Communists seem to have failed to arrest the decline in agricultural production at a relatively high level. The harvest of 1959 probably and the harvests of 1960 and 1961 certainly were grossly inferior to that of 1958. Output during the latter years decreased so much that most agricultural products could not be exported and that scarce foreign exchange had to be spent on grain imports. For lack of detailed information, it is merely possible to hypothesize that decreased agricultural production must have led to decreases in the peasants' own consumption as well as to decreases in state purchases. The implications of this plausible hypothesis are readily apparent. Decreased purchases of agricultural raw materials should have led to decreased production in light industry, to decreased supplies of consumer goods for nonagricultural labor force and peasants alike, and thus probably also to decreased work efforts and to decreased productivity in all branches. Increases in the exports of nonagricultural consumer goods in an attempt to substitute for decreased agricultural exports could have aggravated the situation further. Decreased imports of modern means of production could have affected all industries, depending on the pattern of allocation.

The failure of the Chinese Communists to stop the decline of agricultural output in time must have been of great importance. In order to console the Chinese people after the "great leap forward" had proved to be a disaster in many respects, increases in the level of consumption to unprecedented heights would have been most appropriate. Yet, for lack of adequate reserves and because of inferior levels of production, such a measure was beyond reach. Short of it, the Chinese Communists could attempt to reorient production as much to consumer requirements as various constraints on short-run changes would permit. While there is little information and much speculation on the actual state of the economy, there are the "Ten Assignments" which summarize recent policy in this direction aptly: First, the government called for an increase of agricultural output and particularly of grains, cotton, and oil seeds. Second, it demanded a rational allocation of light industrial and heavy industrial output, so that the production of daily necessities in particular could be increased further. Third, it required a contraction of the "basic investment front" and a redirection of materials, equipment, and manpower into spheres where they were needed most. Fourth, it decreed that segments of the urban population and labor force be sent back to the countryside to participate in rural production and strengthen the "agricultural front." To be moved first were those who had come to the cities recently—that is, during the "great leap forward." Fifth, it required a transfer of all unused stocks and funds to spheres where they were needed most at the present in "adjustment work." Sixth, it appealed for good work in the planned marketing of commodities and for improvements in the urban market supply situation. Seventh, it called for ardent fulfillment of the assignments in regard to foreign trade. Eighth, it demanded adjustments in cultural, educational, scientific, hygienic, and other activities and improvements in the quality of their work. Ninth, it appealed for thorough efforts at "building the country diligently and efficiently," for ardently economizing expenditures and increasing income. Tenth, it demanded further advances in planning and good work in establishing priorities for the various sectors of the economy, in the order: agriculture, light industry, heavy industry.

To conclude, then, the Chinese Communists tried to cope with the aftermath of the "great leap forward" by calling for a strategic retreat. It involved decreases in the rate of accumulation and probably changes in the pattern of distribution in the interest of increasing "material incentives," at least relatively. It also involved attempts at rationalization in the interest of increasing efficiency. In particular, the Chinese Communists liquidated a mass of marginal enterprises and activities which had sprung up during the "great leap forward," largely in connection with the implementation of the "new methods" in agriculture. Men and resources which had been tied up in these ventures were reallocated to productive activities that held out greater promise. The state of disorganization required large-scale inventory-taking for this purpose. Because of the apparent extent of the economic decline during the "three hard years," however, it can also be surmised that the decreases in capital formation and the changes in the patterns of factor and product allocation were particularly extreme. In the interest of reconciliation, the Chinese Communists can be expected to have furthered consumption at the expense of capital formation to a greater extent than that which they envisage for the future. For this reason, it seems proper to probe briefly into the prospects for the future.

SOME PROSPECTS FOR THE FUTURE

Any speculation about the future economic policy of the Chinese Communists is necessarily precarious. A few developments seem to be sufficiently evident, however, to serve as premises for some inferences. Generally, it appears that the combined experiences of the "great leap forward" and of the "three hard years" have not led the Chinese Communists to question the wisdom of Marxist-Leninist-Maoist doctrine and its implications for the basic pattern of economic development. As in the past, they seem to adhere to the notion that in order to develop the economy as rapidly as possible, all "labor power" has to be mobilized. This understanding is evident in the facts that they began to institute urban communes cautiously at a time when the agricultural disaster was apparent already, and that they have not yet "reformed" the rural communes to the extent of relieving female laborers of communal work obligations. Also as in the past, they seem to be convinced that the labor force cannot be trained intensively at once in their entirety and that modern means of production cannot be provided at once for all economic activities. Consequently, we may also surmise that the strategy of "walking on two legs" has not been abandoned in principle, either, and that the problem of future policy is largely a question of how to minimize the bad *limp* of the past that made the leaping giant fall.

In dealing with this problem, the Chinese Communists face a situation which is similar in many ways to that of 1957. The labor force on which they can draw is relatively larger due to communeization, but it can grow primarily only by means of natural increases. Its quality is superior due to training and experiences which have accumulated in the meantime, but more remains to be done than has been done in the past. Labor-force motivation is in all likelihood inferior at the present. Their means of production have increased greatly, but there remains still a severe shortage of capital. Improvements in the means of production cannot be assessed easily, since advances in design must be balanced against evident wear and tear during the "great leap forward." Their dependence on imports of means of production seems to have decreased, but by no means completely so. In addition, they can be certain now that improvements in "indigenous methods" do not provide an easy solution to their problems.

Given these constraints and the Marxist approach to problems of political economy, it should be expected that improvements in the "quality of labor" will be emphasised even more than in the past as the major determinant of economic growth. Consequently, formal training programs as well as informal mass learning are likely to expand increasingly. In view of past lessons, it should also be anticipated that at least at the beginning, learning efforts will be induced and sustained by means of "material incentives" rather than by ideological exhortations. Since it seems probable, too, that any future effort—that is, laboring as well as learning—will require stronger material stimulants than in the past, consumption can be expected to increase in relative terms over the latter fifties, thus implying a relatively low rate of accumulation for the near future.

In distributing the relatively smaller accumulation funds on the major branches of the economy, the Chinese Communists will have to find a new solution for a problem that confronted them previously as well. So long as "nature has not been conquered," there is reason to expect a low marginal efficiency of capital in agriculture proper, due to the whims of nature. Agricultural misfortunes can be alleviated to some extent by primitive accumulation, but an adequate degree of control over floods and drought, insect pests and plant diseases, and so forth, requires "Western methods" and heavy investment in dams and dikes, chemical industry, and so forth. It is likely that in consequence of their past experiences, the Chinese Communists will expand and accelerate projects of this nature and that they will change the pattern of basic construction in accordance with this shift in emphasis. It is also clear, however, that so long as they do not rely strongly on foreign trade to provide the investment goods which are needed for this purpose, they will continue to face the constraint that in order to develop agriculture by "Western methods," they will have to develop first various producer-goods industries to a greater extent. In view of their evident export problems, therefore, they could well be led to continue during the near future their past policy of concentrating modern means of production on the industrial sector and of encouraging the development of agriculture proper by means of improvements in techniques rather than by means of heavy investment. In all likelihood, such improvements will be brought about in a more cautious way than in the past.

Obviously, the traditional agricultural policy will yield the traditionally small increases in agricultural output and, therefore, in the supply of agricultural products for processing by industry. In order to reconcile this outcome with the requirement that consumer-goods supplies to the labor force must be increased in order to induce and sustain adequate efforts, the Chinese Communists will have little choice in their allocation of the remaining investment funds. They will have to develop relatively rapidly consumer-goods industries which do not depend strongly on agricultural raw materials for the purpose of supplementing consumer goods of agricultural origin. As a consequence, investment in heavy industry is likely to decrease and to change in structure in the interest of developing rapidly the appropriate branches of consumer-goods industries. It appears that the chemical industry will also be particularly important in this respect.

In distributing the consumer goods so as to facilitate production, the Chinese Communists are likely to find that they will have to subsidize agriculture increasingly in order to minimize peasant dissatisfaction with small increases in output and thus in their own consumption, as well as with increasing urban-rural earnings differentials which are likely to result from material inducements to learning in combination with heavy investment in industry. Within the modern sector, earnings differentials are likely to change in favor of skilled labor and in favor of the new priority industries.

Finally, as a result of increasing domestic consumption requirements, exports of consumer goods are likely to decrease at least relatively to consumer-goods production, with the result that limits will be placed on imports. It would appear that the increased emphasis on learning and the change to consumer-goods production will ameliorate their effects on the economy to some extent.

While it could yield significant "improvements in the people's level of living" in the longer run, the above pattern of policy is not likely to change the state of affairs substantially in the immediate future. At the same time, it would sacrifice the development of heavy industry to some extent. Therefore, the Chinese Communists might well be tempted to endanger this strategy in the interest of rapid economic growth by overemphasising rural subsidiary activities as a substitute for urban industrial activities in consumer-goods production, and by resorting once again to excessive indoctrination as a substitute for supplies. From the point of view of those who have to bear with them, then, one should hope that the Chinese Communists have learned their lesson well. . . .

11

THE INTELLECTUAL
REVOLUTION IN CHINA

Joseph R. Levenson

If we begin this story with the Opium War (1839-1842) and the
first set of "Unequal Treaties" (1842-1845), we are assuming that
the Western world (in the first instance, England) was the catalyst
of revolution. But the Chinese communists, in whose triumph the
revolution culminated, have quite another view of it. They are
committed to periodization on universal Marxist lines, which would
have Chinese capitalism and socialism, in necessary sequence, issu-
ing from a feudal matrix; these stages could not depend on the
interference of an outside civilization. Rather, the West connived
with Confucian "feudalists" to press down on a budding democracy that was poised against them both. Chinese history on its own
developed in a way not just its own: That is the primary communist statement, with equal stress on both of its halves, which, taken
together, bespeak the equivalence of China and Europe. And the
communists claim title to the equivalence because they are the ones,
"antifeudal" and "anti-imperialist" at the same time, who place
themselves at the point of balance between a rejected Confucian
China and a resisted modern West.

But what put the search for equivalence into Chinese history, not
in its communist phase alone but in the century preceding it? Cultural self-questioning, progressively deepening, left thinkers unsure
of their Chinese identity, as Confucian authority yielded to Western

Dr. Levenson, Professor of History, University of California, Berkeley,
is the author of *Liang Ch'i-ch'ao and the Mind of Modern China* (1953)
and of *Confucian China and its Modern Fate: the Problem of Intellectual
Continuity* (1958). This article is reprinted, with permission, from *The
University of Toronto Quarterly*, Vol. 30, No. 3 (April 1961), 258-272.
Copyright © 1961 by the University of Toronto Press.

authority and Chinese history seemed to be draining off into Western channels. A series of innovators tried to secure the continuity of Chinese history, even as they responded to circumstances impairing it with new ideas belying it. Actually, so many Chinese may have felt so strongly about the autonomous generation of their modern values because autonomy was in doubt. More than likely, Chinese communism has come to the fore just because of the foreign invasions—which broke the older civilization and set off the drive for compensation—and not in spite of them, in train of inevitable historical progress. Explicitly, a communist view of the past century may tell us more about the eye of the beholder than about the nature of the past beheld. But implicitly, the communist explanation is a vital clue to the past, such a past that it culminated in the wide acceptance of just this eccentric view.

When the Manchu official Ch'i-ying negotiated the end of the Opium War in 1842, he flattered the British to their faces while describing them contemptuously in memorials to the throne. As he explained it to his emperor, the British, now properly "pacified," were too barbarous to realize that they were barbarians; conventional assumptions of Chinese superiority, therefore, would only irritate them, and these had better be left unstated in the official documents. Here Ch'i-ying, with an extreme assertion, in private, of Chinese superiority, was screening his inability to assert it in public. But when Chinese had to condescend in silence, it meant that they were beginning to see, dimly, a new kind of foreigner confronting them (Ch'i-ying himself, an assimilable Manchu, was the old kind). They were on their way to recognizing a new kind of China as well—no longer a world, but a nation in the world.

The road to nationhood was paved with new inventions. Their technology made these foreigners now not only victorious over the Chinese in war but equipped to exploit victory from a distance. Unlike the Manchus, modern Europeans had no need to assimilate to China. And the Chinese, unable to take them in, were just as unable to throw them out as long as the technological gap endured. Thus, from the 1840's on, a line of "self-strengtheners" brought Western technology more and more into their circle of acceptance, and they were drawn inexorably through merely military science to the industrial and political. The perimeter of the purely indigenous values shrank, even for bureaucratic Confucianists who longed to keep their social prominence and cultural distinction. While they defended the ever more narrowly defined "Chinese essence," the same West which gave them the insidious tools of defense—a merely useful technology, as it was supposed to be—was transforming an old social type, the agrarian rebel, into a proto-revolutionary, and creating a new social type, the legally protected capitalist, in the treaty ports. New roads to social prominence, new content to cultural distinction began to threaten the old *élite*, even as the latter, in its own right, was shifting the ground of Confucianism, converting it from substance of education for life and action, to symbol of China's individuality.

The agrarian rebels were the Taipings (1850-1864). They flouted Confucianism with a garbled Christianity, part of the Western intellectual penetration. And they were pushed over the edge of rebellion by the Western economic penetration, which aggravated endemic social bitterness to a new intensity. Intellectual apostasy underscored this bitterness. Literati-officials and landlords, almost unanimously loyal to the Ch'ing, the Manchu dynasty, damned the rebels as seceders from cultural China. For what the Taipings proclaimed was a national China, in which an ethnically foreign dynasty, however Confucian in its sympathies and culturally legitimate, was nationally illegitimate.

The dynasty survived for a while; the Taipings went down. But the intellectual revolution of the twentieth century was anticipated in the Taipings' fusion of cultural iconoclasm and political nationalism. And their fusion of cultural iconoclasm and rudimentary class-analysis (the Taipings' animus toward landlords being inseparable from their anti-Confucianism) foreshadowed the fate of that revolution: pre-emption by the communists.

Along with their religious novelties, the Taipings found other things to admire in Western culture. Hung Jen-kan, for example, an influential cousin of the "Heavenly King" of the Taipings, recommended sweeping changes in Chinese customs and institutions. Calligraphy and painting were not important, he said; railroads, steamships, barometers, and thermometers were the kinds of things to admire. Superficially, in making positive recommendations like these, the rebels seemed akin to the literati-official "self-strengtheners," who also could be enthusiastic about ships and trains. But there was a real difference between them, not just in the degree of zeal for modernization but in the nature of the objective. The Taipings sought alternatives to the official values of Chinese culture, while the officials—at least those who were relatively open-minded, not obscurantist—looked rather for supplements, material shields to the spiritual heart of a culture.

What the Taipings showed was the mark of alienation. A Chinese could not disown so many old sancta of Chinese culture, simply and ruthlessly, unless he felt that what he was shedding was not of himself. He could feel himself Chinese, but then the rejected culture would be relegated solely to a class, for which Confucianism would stand as ideology, no longer as the central idea of civilization in the large. On the other hand, the anti-Taiping literati who owned that culture (in the sense that Confucian high culture had long been connected with high standing in the Confucian state, and in the sense that literati provided the historians of the culture and most of the record which the histories enshrined) were concerned to defend it, not discard it. They had to look on the culture not as the emblem of a class but of a total, distinctive people.

And so the fatal stain of relativism began to spread over Confucian culture which had hitherto been prized as civilization in the abstract, not as *a* civilization in a world with others. Even now, in the latter half of the nineteenth century, Confucianists facing Taipings, or only just rid of them, did not lower the flag; ostensibly, their Confucian avowals were still absolute and universal. But when Confucianists were shocked into self-consciousness by those *indigenous* barbarians, the Taipings, whose disavowals of Confucianism removed them morally from the Chinese world, the foreign barbarians assumed another aspect. They were not just, theoretically, aspirants to Confucian culture, potentially Chinese but handicapped by their physical remove from the center of the world. They were genuine rivals, able, obviously, to pose cultural alternatives even to Chinese. And that very shock which made the literati, facing inward, fix Confucian culture as the possession of *all* Chinese made them, facing outward, define it as the possession of all *Chinese*. When they insisted on cultural solidarity in order to paste over the cracks in social solidarity at home, they endowed it with implications just as defensive abroad. Confucian China faced the world, instead of containing it.

The question was, rather, whether the Western world would contain China. Not only rebels, as we have seen, but would-be defenders of Confucianism were ready to see Western culture in some of its aspects make a mark in China. Missionaries introduced a wider and wider range of secular Western learning, and to some extent Chinese officials collaborated with them or took fire from their ex-

ample. Li Hung-chang, for instance, memorialized in 1863 for a
school of languages and science. He observed ruefully that for
twenty years a fair number of foreigners had been studying the Chinese language and could read Chinese Classics, histories, and state
papers, while there had been practically no corresponding activity
on the Chinese side. There was something ominous about this memorial: A situation which once would have been deemed a normal
one and grounds for complacency (foreigners aspiring to the higher
things, Chinese serene in their self-sufficiency) now was cause for
alarm. Should the culture be left unmodified, the nation would be
endangered. For when Chinese learning was becoming not necessarily an end but a tactical weapon for Westerners, Chinese indif-
ference to Western learning was a dreamlike vestigial fancy.

Syncretism was called for in the waking world. Somehow, if one
had any feeling at all for the preservation of Confucian values, the
latter had to be harmonized with the new knowledge. Li Hung-
chang and the other self-strengtheners deprecated their Western
borrowings as means, not ends, but the "means" too obviously were
sweeping all but the rhetoric before them. Knowledge of the means
was becoming so essential that it was reducing the Chinese learning
to historical significance, though this learning was the ostensible
essence that the means were supposed to protect. It remained for a
group near the end of the century, the "Reformers," to try to natu-
ralize the foreign learning by bringing it within Confucianism, not
just suffering it to serve. In particular, the disastrous Sino-Japanese
war of 1894-1895 convinced them that mere sufferance of the Western learning was not enough. A Confucianism that walled off the
great subjects of modern thought stripped itself of relevance and
China of her defenses. The Reformers persuaded themselves that
this was unnecessary and illegitimate, for what they valued they had
truly inherited; Confucius, correctly understood, the orthodox read-
ing of the Classics being properly amended, gave a Chinese warrant
to science, democracy, and the theory of historical progress.

The Reformers had a brief moment of political influence (the
"Hundred Days," summer, 1898), but by and large Confucianists
in office made their social plans abortive, while Confucianists in
commitment rejected their emendations to the textual tradition. In
fact, the modernist Confucianism of the Reformers could only be a
way station to either a modernization under non-Confucian aus-
pices on the one hand, or to a Confucianism ranged against the
Western, modern influence on the other. For the academic or-

thodoxy which the Reformers assailed had been responsible for maintaining Confucius' reputation as a sage. The Confucius of the traditional Confucianists was the Confucius who mattered historically, and the Reformers' zeal to rehabilitate him as a popular champion (among other things), to absolve him of responsibility for the later authoritarianism, was excessive; if Confucius had not been taken over by literati-officials of the imperial state, he would never have been so prominent in history as to invite such modern attention. The only Confucius whose imprimatur could matter was the Confucius of a society which the Confucian Reformers were ready to undercut.

Actually, to undercut it, their recommendations were not required. Rather, a Western challenge, social and intellectual, was already irresistible, and their Confucian-Western syncretism was not an incitement but a response. Without any Confucian sanction, Western culture would still be making inroads; it was Confucius' influence in China that was at stake, not Western influence, and it was the Confucian side of the Confucian Westernizers, not the Western side, that needed the syncretism. Chinese thinkers in general needed it, or some more viable intellectual formula, to harmonize their Chinese attachments with their awareness of the West.

The final proof that the search for harmony could not be avoided came with the Boxer Movement of 1900. In this xenophobic rising, Chinese peasants and Ch'ing protegees among the officials tried pathetically to drown out Western influence as a discordant note, and bring China back to her lost aloneness. Boxerism was a terrible simplification of China's Western problem; this desperate, last illusion of triumph of the will over practical power had to be tried to be dispelled. The Boxer Movement was the last paroxysm of solid antiforeignism in Chinese history.

It was solid in a double sense. First, it was absolutely opposed not only to Western political purposes but to all Western culture. And second, there was a great degree of Chinese class solidarity in this particular response to the West. But the Western intrusion had made it inevitable that Chinese culture should be dynamically changed and Chinese class relations embittered. After the Boxer hopelessness, antiforeignism yielded to nationalism, with all its potential affinity for cultural innovation. And instead of Chinese social solidarity against the outside world we find decades of revolution, with one or another Chinese group being scorned as "running dogs" of one foreign bloc or another.

After 1900, in its last decade, the dynasty turned from sponsoring the utterly discredited Boxer type of obscurantism to encouraging, modestly, new social forces that conceivably might strengthen the state. Patents, company law, industrial schools, and tax reductions were instituted in an effort to nurture industry for the state's defense. It was an effort, in the self-strengthening spirit, to protect the old order. Yet, the means were hard to reconcile with a basic premise of the old order: Traditionally, business was not something to bolster the state apparatus, but something on which the state's officials battened. The mandarinate's timid encouragement of industry was an attempt to prolong its life. But as long as its life was prolonged, there was a drag on industry; and to the extent that industry resisted the drag, the mandarin order was threatened.

The same ambiguity plagued the regime in another of its recourses, the sponsorship of foreign study, especially in Japan. In lieu of the ineffective old thought of the Boxers, modern thought which the Boxers hated had to be mastered, but in the end this was hardly an intellectual expedient that could fortify the Ch'ing. For the dynasty was as vulnerable now as in Taiping days to Chinese nationalism—more vulnerable, really, since even the literati's education in Confucian culture (which took the curse off Manchu foreignness) was falling into abeyance. And nationalism ran rampant in Chinese student circles in Japan; so much was to be learned in Japan which could not be assimilated into traditional Chinese culture that the antitraditional potentialities of nationalism commended it to the students. If it was nationally useful, one could legitimately choose the culturally unorthodox. Both reason and emotion favored the choice. Rationally, as a nationalist one could justify innovation if it strengthened the nation. And emotionally, if the nation, not the tradition, was supposed to matter, one could be soothed while discerning tradition's decay. Rather than contemplate China as a defeated traditional culture, there were those who preferred to envision it as a culturally changed victorious nation.

Therefore, the Manchus, trying to conjure up strength to save themselves from a traditional dynastic overthrow, invited a modern one. Chinese nationalism, at least in part, was a concomitant of Manchu reform policy, and nationalism hit the Manchus in two ways. First, it arraigned them as foreign usurpers and, worse still, usurpers in power during years and years of Chinese defeats. And second, the iconoclastic implications of nationalism, like the patriotic ones, made bad news for the Ch'ing. Many nationalists were just as ready to overthrow the old institution of the throne as, say, the old institution of foot-binding.

In 1911 and 1912 the overthrow was achieved and the Chinese republican era began. Almost from the start it soured the hopes of its partisans. Nothing seemed changed socially—a grave disappointment to the evolutionary expectations of Sun Yat-sen, leader of the Kuomintang, the party of republican nationalists. Sun had looked on a republic as the latest thing in politics, inherently better than monarchy (constitutional or not). But here was the Chinese Republic floundering into fragments, its people still subject to the old exploitations, while its "strong man," Yüan Shih-k'ai, was scheming to wreck it entirely.

And yet, something had changed. The political and social revolutions seemed hollow, but a cultural revolution had been seriously furthered; when the Ch'ing fell, the monarchical mystique seemed drained, and all manner of old traditions were emptied with it. Genuinely new thought jarred with its spuriously new political environment. The abortive revolution of 1911, abortive but not meaningless, was really part of a process of revolution. It had not yet worked itself out. When easy expectations of a predetermined advancement were dispelled, the field was cleared for a revolution with iron content, not airy verbiage.

And it was a stage in revolution, not just a pseudo-revolutionary fiasco, in another way. The Manchu question was buried. Society did not seem to improve (the revolution *might* seem mere fiasco), but the Manchus were no longer available as a lightning rod for nationalistic passions. The latter could no longer be diverted from their always potential target, *Chinese* responsibility for China's low estate. After 1912, unmistakably, Chinese society and culture themselves, not whatever the Manchus were supposed to have done to them, came under coldest scrutiny. To the intellectual leaders of the "Chinese Renaissance" (around *New Youth,* founded 1915, certain other periodicals, and the "May Fourth Movement" of 1919), the Manchus were dead, and the Chinese paladins of traditional culture were nakedly exposed. That most untraditional of Chinese conflicts, the conflict of generations, was openly encouraged.

A new literature began to emerge as one expression of this conflict, an expression in both form and content. In content, the literature was permeated by concern with family tensions, both political and personal—crabbed age and youth ranged against each other on questions of public social action and private freedom for the emotional life. In form, the literature exemplified the conflict in its very language, a vernacular Chinese instead of the classical language which, by the old standards, was the only medium for respectable expression. The rise of vernacular seemed to its advocates one of their points of contact with the European Renaissance, which the "May Fourth" generation chose to exalt as a harbinger of the day of the young, not a revival of antiquity.

Actually, the very drive to construct this "Renaissance" analogy compromised its validity. The analogy was supposed to extend to nationhood. But there was a vast distinction between several nations discovering their identities within Europe (via vernacular literatures, and so on) and a single nation *redefining* its identity as China. Substitution of national for cultural loyalty was implicit in the young Chinese nationalism (not in the Western specimens), and the content of the nationalists' "New Culture Movement" was so largely drawn from the West that an impulse to lay the spectre of debt was almost irresistible. Parallel development to scientific and democratic cultures—down a Classic-Mediaeval-Renaissance-Modern paradigm, as one possibility—was a comforting assumption. But the comfort had to be sought because the parallel could not really be found.

This flaw in the cultural heart of Chinese nationalism broke it into extremes. A central position of noncommunist antitraditionalism was a weak position, for the West seemed too intrusive. Intellectually, a move to the left, to communism, gave a sanction to modernization that seemed emotionally less expensive, on three counts. First, if science was one of the new values, then it seemed appropriate to locate it in the Marxist paradigm of historical progress, since Marxism stressed its scientific pretensions. Then, this very historicism enabled Marxists to relativize the values they felt outworn; where an absolute curse on the tradition (like much of the "May Fourth" invective) might seem to outrage the Chinese personality, the relegation of tradition to its own era would save it for China, yet gratifyingly bury it as a live option. And finally, the Marxist critique had just as fine a cutting edge for modern Europe as for modern China. Revolution everywhere was recommended. Instead of a simple (but difficult) liberal admiration for the West and impatience with an unreconstructed China, communism could offer even-handed hostility to "imperialists" abroad and "feudalists" at home.

Of course, the communist refuge from the pain of modernization could not be open to everyone. Conservative nationalism was the other intellectual pole after "May Fourth." This was a post-Confucian China; it cost something to be a Chinese thinker in a world of Western thought. If communism made compensation for the loss of tradition, how did an anticommunist nationalism face the loss?

It reintegrated traditionalism into iconoclasm. This sounds paradoxical, since Chinese nationalism, as we have suggested, depended on the waning of tradition. Yet, this paradox is a central fact in modern Chinese history and a key to its complexity.

One must insist that in conservative nationalism, as in any other, the untraditional was always there, at least latently. In the political struggles of the 1920's, just after "May Fourth," genuine traditionalists, those with a primary commitment to tradition, were antinationalist. Either they favored war-lord interests against Sun Yat-Sen, his Kuomintang nationalists, and their provisional allies, the communists (1924-1927); or they opposed the war lords in a totally reactionary way, identifying the scourge of warlordism with the scourge of the Republic and looking back nostalgically to the old imperial days. The lines were drawn in the early 1920's: Political nationalism and cultural iconoclasm were aligned together against political antinationalism (that is, war lords, some of them with foreign backing) and cultural conservatism. The alliance of Kuomintang and communists, however ephemeral politically, was culturally valid. There was a natural bond between them, as *new men,* all of them new.

Then what distinguished Kuomintang from communists? If at heart they agreed on cultural iconoclasm, their disagreement had to be social. Kuomintang adherents were eager to prevent the expropriation they foresaw if the communists prospered. Therefore, they opposed communist class-analysis of society, since that augured so ill for them. And this social cleavage had cultural implications, for one of the fruits of communist class-analysis was a new version of the old Taiping approach, the attribution of certain traditional values to a ruling class alone. This intellectual attitude, together with others, mentioned above (like satisfaction in seeing the West as well as China consigned to revolution), was what made it emotionally possible for Chinese communists to desert tradition.

But this revolutionary medicine was unavailable to nationalists who would be ruined by revolution. Hence, for both polemical (as an argument against social opponents) and psychological purposes (as emotional sustenance for themselves), nationalists reintegrated traditionalism into their nationalism. Socially, tradition was useful to nationalists as anticommunists; denying that class-war should exist, they held that all Chinese belonged together as Chinese, and distinctly Chinese values, transcending social divisions, would be a cultural cement. And psychologically, tradition was necessary to nationalists as noncommunists, barred by their social requirements from the communist means of renouncing a moribund system. They were nationalist enough to feel estrangement from their traditional culture, but the communist brand of compensation was socially impossible. Therefore, their only way to treat the malaise that alienation bred was to deny the alienation.

Already, ever since the first iconoclastic stirrings of the nationalism leading to 1911 and 1919, the defense of tradition had tended to be romantically conservative, not rationalistically conservative in the primary Confucian sense. That is, the authentic Confucian case for traditionalism had been turned into a traditionalist case for Confucianism—a Confucianism rendered as modern, as "transvalued," as iconoclasm itself. As a component of conservative nationalism, militating against radical social change, neo-traditionalism (Confucian "national essence" and all) testified as eloquently as anything else to the thoroughly post-Confucian nature of republican Chinese history.

The tribute paid by conservative nationalists to old official values —even while these conservatives were as finally divorced from real tradition as the communists were—exposed them to more of the communist class critique; it was this critique in the first place which had elicited the traditionalistic (but not traditional) response. When the Kuomintang labored traditional values instead of living in a pure and simple commitment to them, this encouraged desertions on the class-analysis grounds which the communists owned and which the anticommunists were precluded from accepting. Accordingly, the Kuomintang's pseudo-Confucian "New Life Movement" in the 1930's was doomed to inanition. As traditionalism became more transparently a social device, it lost its claim to philosophical respect.

When the Kuomintang lost its grip after World War II, the Communist Party, not the "Democratic League" or any other "Third Force" grouping, took full power. There were many good political reasons why it ended like this; one could explain in political terms the impotence of the liberals in recent Chinese history. Intellectual history is no substitute for political explanation here, but it is a corroboration, or as much a part of a rich complex as the Taiping case affords. If intellectual revolution in modern China has taken a communist turn, not a liberal antitraditionalist one, it is not just that communists won politically and laid down an intellectual line. There were circumstances in Chinese culture that led to the line— intellectual circumstances leading as logically to a communist polity as political circumstances led to a communist credo.

A Christian credo, also, had been offered to China in the modern period. Christian missions had deeply affected the breakdown of the old order. But the fate of Christianity vis-à-vis Marxism in China paralleled the fate of liberal Westernizers in their confrontation with communists. With a glance at the problem of Chinese Christianity, let us recapitulate the grammar of Marxist assent.

There were particular difficulties in nineteenth-century proselytizing. Chinese were baffled at the deluge of scriptures having so few points of contact with their own culture, and the church was embroiled in Chinese resentment of the "unequal treaties" which had been wrested by force and were mainstays of the missions. However, with the discrediting of the Boxer xenophobia (particularly fierce in its anti-Christianity), there came a time of promise to the missions. Moods changed in the 1920's; nationalist student youth made both an intellectual and political assault on the missions, despite a considerable missionary effort to shake free of embarrassing associations. With the rise of the communist threat, missionaries and nationalists (that is, the Kuomintang, anticommunist nationalists) came closer together. With the communist triumph, the missions shared in the nationalist debacle.

So much for a bare historical sketch. But the historical question posed by it is nothing less than how it became possible for Chinese minds to drift from historical Chinese values. Right from the start, missionaries had feared that the materially useful elements of Western culture which they brought to China might be adopted without (as they considered it) the spiritual essence. But why should they face this prospect? We recall that there were Chinese, too, concerned with the matter-spirit dichotomy, but with a reversed emphasis: For conservative reformers, the problem seemed one of hedging a *Chinese* spiritual essence with merely useful Western material. Such a concern for Chinese equivalence with the materially irresistible West, we have suggested, has been discernible in all shades of modern Chinese thought, and Christianity in China, probably inevitably, was its victim. Christianity's role was vicarious. Chinese came to require it, not as something to be believed in but as something to be rejected.

That is, as an ultimate faith, empirically undemonstrable, Christianity was *rejectable,* in a way that modern science (which Christianity helped to introduce) was not; so Christianity (the West as "Christian civilization") became ballast to unload, to right the balance when industrialism (the West as "industrial civilization") had to be taken on. The obvious indictments of missionaries—on counts like cultural obtuseness, interference in litigation, or just simple foreignness—make failures plausible for this time or that, but in themselves, uninterpreted in the wider cultural context, they do not account for the dynamic in Chinese anti-Christianity. This dynamic was the change from the charge of "antitraditional" to the charge of "antimodern."

If we dwell on the fact that the Boxers hated a foreign technology as well as a foreign religion, we see more than the mere occasions of the Christian dilemma. For it is the Boxers' antimodern, not their anti-Christian, paroxysm that strikes us as fantastic, and this because we sense that Western technology must get through in the end. The Boxer rage against Christianity seems fanatic but not fantastic; there are no historical factors which make its rejection unthinkable. Boxer (and Confucian-intellectual) antimodernism faded like any illusion, but the malaise which called it forth was real, and the Boxers' one *possible* cultural balm, defeat of Christianity, almost had to come when antimodernism had to go. The continuity of Chinese history, vindication of Chinese self-respect, seemed to be at stake. Christians, who had tried for a long time, some of them, to confound Confucianists with science and thus to level the Chinese wall against themselves as Western, succeeded so well that they failed, and found themselves just "mediaevals" disqualified by "moderns."

Seen thus, both the Chinese and Christian predicaments had a poignancy about them. The missionaries were in a maze: Chinese need of reassurance was such that in whatever direction the Christians headed—towards accommodation to historical Chinese culture or towards renovation—they were equally lost. One can find tactical flaws in the Christian approaches, but these were not the determinants of failure. If one assumes so, he implies that Christianity, not communism, might have won the chance to make the new Chinese culture.

So it may, later, when the conditions of Chinese intellectual choice are far from what they have been in the last hundred years; the future is not prejudged. Yet, for our own day, the forces which favored a Marxist breakthrough in modern China were the very ones which made for the Christian impasse. One ought not to see the defeat of Christianity in China as simply a corollary of the communist victory (communism being anti-Christian), and then look for the causes of communist triumph irrespective of Christianity's place in Chinese history. Christianity did not wait in the wings to see who prevailed, communists or Kuomintang, and only lose when its own sworn enemy won. Rather, Christianity, in retrospect, seems made for the scaffold in modern China, and for the same reasons that Marxism has taken the throne.

What about communism in prospect? Such episodes as the "Hundred Flowers" outburst of criticism of the communist regime (1957) may make it appear that the intelligentsia, corralled by main force, is in the communist state but not of it. Perhaps, after all, this is a Chinese intelligentsia in a living tradition, with the latest version of an old Confucian detachment from autocracy. May the disenchantment of the students, largely educated under communism, point towards the end of the communist intellectual appeal and the rehabilitation of the tradition it supplanted?

The communist appeal may certainly dwindle, but no "Chinese essence" is likely to be refurbished. If intellectuals now are tools, merely used (hence subject to harassment) by those who run the state, the state in which intellectuals were ends, the Confucian state, had been deserted by just these modern intellectuals or their recent forbears. They do not, in short, represent an unmoving, perennial element in Chinese society, whose fate in contemporary China can be explained by reference to state directives, an outside force. If China has changed to the extent that such a state exists, the intelligentsia has changed with it. Contemporary intellectuals are not outside the system, resisting or bending to force; their character helps to account for the system's existence. If they come to threaten its existence, they will do so not because the precommunist order is so alive that its faithful ones triumph, but so dead that defectors from it may split among themselves.

Still, they really are, really were defectors. It is sometimes suggested that the communist regime is a new dynasty, with grand old Confucian institutions: bureaucracy, Classics, and a True Way. However titillating, this paradox ought to be set aside. Chinese communism is no Confucian masquerade. "Anti-Western" means one thing in cold-war terminology, other things in Opium War or Boxer parlance. This is not Confucianism prospering in communist guise, because Chinese communism—offering itself as compensation to heirs with a vanishing heritage—responds (and corresponds) to Confucian impoverishment.

And if communism is a response to this historical break, it is hardly the fruit of unbroken historical growth. Indeed, there has been an intellectual revolution in modern China. But China has not just revolved back to her starting point (wherever this paper may be), nor moved onward and upward, driven from within, along lines laid down in antiquity. Western history has tangled the lines.

12

TRADITION AND EXPERIMENT IN MODERN CHINESE LITERATURE

Yi=tsi M. Feuerwerker

Unlike most labels in literary history, "Modern Chinese Literature" is one that can be applied without any ambiguity. It began with a revolution whose date—1917—has been fixed with comfortable precision. The literary movement which followed has been highly self-conscious with well-formulated programs that indicate an unequivocal break with the past. While it may be customary for every literary movement to define its position through assumed antitheses to its immediate past, challenging the literary historian to trace the inevitable inheritance from tradition, modern Chinese literature, in both program and performance, has been unmistakably antitraditional.

If antitraditionalism is a definite feature of modern Chinese literature, it is less easy to define the particular tradition that required revolt, the specific direction of subsequent development, and the complex processes of change itself. Certain answers can best be sought in the sequel to that precipitate rejection of tradition by the "Literary Revolution," in the subsequent decade 1920-1930 when the new writers were conscientiously attempting to "create" a new literature and debating the problem of tradition in the light of these efforts. It was an articulate and polemical period, during which diverse literary schools contributed conflicting programs; but in 1930, with the formation of the League of Leftist Writers, champions of a revolutionary literature for the proletariat, and in spite

In addition to her work on modern Chinese literature and literary personages, Mrs. Feuerwerker has written on the traditional Chinese novel. The present article is reprinted, with permission, from *The University of North Carolina Studies in Comparative Literature*, No. 13 (1955), 107-121. Copyright © 1955 by The University of North Carolina Press.

of continued controversies, a conclusion was reached. Thus these ten years may be said to mark the transition from the overthrow of tradition, through a highly complex period of dissension, to a new but relatively stable and homogeneous literary situation—to the arrival at an outcome, if not at a solution, of the difficult problems raised by antitraditionalism.

A few hazardous but necessary generalizations concerning Chinese traditional literature will have to be made here, while their specific implications will be discussed later in terms of the criticisms and remedies offered by the new writers. Chinese traditional literature was written in the classical language whose cumbersome script had remained unaltered despite phonetic changes and whose syntax had become, in the course of the last two thousand years, more and more distinct from the constantly evolving spoken language. Literary language was thus aurally unintelligible and could be mastered only through the memorization of literary texts. This situation was the result of both the peculiarity of the linguistic medium and the traditional concept of the nature and function of literature. Although literature was regarded as a distinct human activity, it was not autonomous: its aesthetic function was generally subordinate to a social one. The civil service examination system, through which the literati were recruited into the upper bureaucracy, asked for classical literary knowledge and perpetuated the old conventions. Thus granted a definite position in the social scheme, classical literature tended to become a consciously didactic instrument for social values. Since at least the tenth century, however, a subtradition of literature had been growing up. This subtradition, which included the novel and drama, was written in the colloquial language and aimed primarily to provide entertainment for a popular audience. The transformation of popular genres, especially metrical forms, into serious literary conventions was a process of "rebarbarization" which prevented the classical tradition from becoming completely stereotyped. These popular language forms—and it must be remembered that the notable works in these genres were the anonymous products of writers from the literati class—were, nevertheless, not recognized as literature and had neither social nor scholarly standing. The restriction of literary purpose, and the emphasis on imitative writing during the preceding five centuries, made it apparent that the potentialities of the classical language had been exhausted.

The acknowledged literary tradition had reached a stage of exhaustion, but the revolt of the modern literary movement was precipitated mainly through extraliterary interferences, through pressures resulting from social and cultural changes. The Western orientation of modern Chinese literature, if isolated from its historical context, would become incomprehensible. Perhaps any investigation of modern China should begin at 1842 with that drastic encounter with the West, the Opium War. The intensified repetitions of that experience, gun-boat policies and unequal treaties, created a change in the intellectual world. Though scarcely recognizing the Western onslaught for what it was, thoughtful Chinese statesmen who had been involved in dealings with the West were beginning to realize that they had to contend unequally with a rival whose techniques were as formidable as they were unfamiliar. It became distressingly clear that the stability of Chinese society was jeopardized, and that what China had regarded as her cultural superiority over the barbarians—the rest of the world—was being seriously challenged. The adjustment to this new feeling of inadequacy was reluctant and painful. One half-hearted concession, which attempted to accommodate Western learning and yet satisfy Chinese pride by proposing the formula "Chinese learning for the fundamental principles, Western learning for practical application" (*Chung-hsüeh wei t'i, Hsi-hsüeh wei yung*), failed to hold out against either traditionalist or iconoclast in a rapidly deteriorating national situation. Efforts to learn from the West became more positive toward the end of the century: Modern schools were established, students sent abroad, and translations made.

Western literature was first translated on a large scale in the last thirty years of the nineteenth century by Lin Shu (1852-1924). Knowing no English, French, or German, he rendered the oral translations of his assistants into classical Chinese prose. In his record of 156 translations, the European authors who head the list are Rider Haggard and Arthur Conan Doyle. (But note that Tolstoi comes third on the list.) The translation of Dumas' *Camille* enjoyed the greatest success; however, it must be stressed, not because of the novelty of its theme for Chinese readers. At any rate, Lin Shu's works mark the beginning of the wholesale importation of Western literary ideas and products.

As knowledge of the West increased, Chinese intellectuals began active verbal campaigns for modernization. These last years of the nineteenth century witnessed the rise of journalism, the public debate of political issues in language increasingly marked by clarity, logic, and the use of popular idioms. Such activities of a progressive and conscientious intelligentsia to combat social backwardness intensified the demand for a simpler and more wieldy medium of instruction. Experimental proposals for language reform were made. The need for rapid and radical change to meet increasingly urgent demands of a foreign world became so desperate that between 1917 and 1919 all earlier, tentative adaptations and leisurely experiments were swept away in an extreme wave of iconoclasm.

The so-called "Literary Revolution," popularized in the West by a rather misleading term "Literary Renaissance," was, thus, in its early stages, more of a cultural than a strictly literary movement. The rehabilitation of the vernacular was almost immediately effected because of the requirement for a tool to facilitate the absorption and propagation of Western knowledge. Whereas the enlightened statesman of the past century had attempted a reluctant assimilation of Western learning within the Chinese system, the foreign-educated leaders of the Literary Revolution commanded an enthusiastic following with such slogans as "Down with Confucianism" and "Total Westernization." The literary issues involved in these drastic changes were lost sight of, or rather, made subservient to the resounding platform of importing Mr. *Te* and Mr. *Sai*—"Mr. Democracy and Mr. Science"—into China. It seemed obvious then that the wholesale adoption of these two Western ideas, rather crudely understood, would equip China with the means of modernization and bring about also the dissolution of her age-worn traditions.

Not that the attempted extension of the scientific and democratic spirit into the realm of literature was not pretentiously made from the very beginning. Both Ch'en Tu-hsiu (1880-1939) and Hu Shih (1891-1962), the leaders, furnished the revolution with literary slogans. In 1917 Ch'en advocated the overthrow of the "classical, stereotyped, obscurantist" literature of the "aristocrat" and the "recluse" in favor of a "plain and realistic" literature of the "people"; Hu Shih demanded the liberation of the literary language from classical allusion, clichés, rhetorical devices, and called for grammar, content, and directness in language that approximated actual speech. As a medium of instruction the colloquial language was introduced into the elementary schools by a decree of the Ministry of Education in 1920. The Literary Revolution begun but three years earlier could then claim success, but the profound literary issues it set in motion were yet to be fought out for at least the following ten years.

With the acknowledged literary tradition in a stage of exhaustion, and antitraditional forces growing under the pressure of social change to culminate in the Literary Revolution of 1917-1919, both the context and the nature of the literary problems to be discussed in the following period become intelligible. From our perspective, the eventual leftward direction of these discussions was inevitable from the beginning.

The avowed aim of those who debated and wrote during the 1920's was the conscious "creation" of a new Chinese literature. Both the internal and external pressures, as outlined above, that occasioned the demand for a new literature had developed to a point where every writer had to take a stand on the problem of tradition. This matter is unquestionably the most convenient focus from which to view the divergent and yet converging trends of this complex period.

Certain external features of this period should be considered first. It has been estimated that between 1922 and 1925 alone over one hundred literary organizations were formed—and they continued to appear after 1925—each publishing a periodical as an outlet for its writings. Among these, five, which together included all the major writers, deserve to be mentioned for their importance: The Literary Studies Society (*Wen-hsüeh yen-chiu hui*), the Creation Society (*Ch'uang-tsao she*), the Small Talk Society (*Yü-ssu she*), the Crescent Society (*Hsin-yüeh she*), and the League of Leftist Writers (*Tso-i tso-chia lien meng*) formed in 1930. In a time of inadequate copyright protection, harsh government censorship, and extreme economic pressure, these were actually "mutual aid associations" as well as intellectual camps. Some published manifestoes setting forth their particular creeds; others gradually defined, and not a few of them changed, their stands through controversy. A second fact is the youthfulness of the writers. With the notable exception of Lu Hsün (1881-1936), the theorists and practitioners of the new literature were born between 1891 and 1901, and had witnessed the Literary Revolution at a rather "impressionable" age. Moreover, practically all had received their university education in foreign countries. One important group, including Lu Hsün and Kuo Mo-jo (1891-   ), went to Japan where they were exposed to

an active leftist movement; another large group studied in England
or America. Having filled themselves with foreign ideas, both groups
returned to address themselves to a young generation carried away
by the fury and speed of reform and revolution. A third factor has
to do with political history. The uneasy cooperation between the
Nationalist (Kuomintang) Party and the Communists came to an
end in the split of 1927, and was followed by a purge of the radi-
cals. The politically conservative elements had also been increasingly embracing the traditionalist cause, as they could see that
cultural iconoclasm was linked with social protest. Their persecu-
tions only served to make the political and intellectual alternatives
all the more compelling. It was this external pressure that finally
forced Lu Hsün, for example, the most influential writer in modern
Chinese literature, into the leftist camp. Thus the violently polemical nature of the literary debates in a multitude of periodicals, the
comparative youthfulness of the writers, and the political commitment of cultural traditionalism are the external factors that contributed to the final victory of the iconoclastic view of tradition.

The issue was not, however, simply determined externally. Some
of the critical discussions should be examined briefly here. The
"creation" of a new literature was taken up with the underlying
assumption that China's literary past was dead to any further pos-
sibilities of development. If certain writers studied earlier works, it
was not to uphold tradition, but to reassess it, or rather to "salvage"
what there might be of value from the discarded "rubbish heap."
Fruitful investigation into the subtradition of unacknowledged,
popular literature was made by the Literary Studies Society, for
example. Their methodology, self-styled as "scientific," resulted in
illuminating studies of origin and development. Less fruitful in
scholarly results was the suddenly vocal traditionalist reaction to
the new literature during the early 1920's. One group was led by an
official of the warlord Anfu Clique in Peking and could be neatly
disposed of by the epithet "feudalistic." Another group had its center at the Tung-nan University in Nanking and consisted of returned students who had been exposed to the influences of Irving
Babbitt; their main arguments were based on an equation of traditional ethical and cultural values—often Confucian—with "neo-
Humanism." The battle was from the beginning a losing one,
merely winning for them from Lu Hsün the name "fake antiques."
One of the most provocative rediscoveries of modern Western criticism, that the writer inevitably begins with an inherited tradition

which he reinterprets in terms of his own present, was too subtle and complex an argument to be exploited effectively even by the Chinese traditionalists—how much less was it available to those who were rebelling against tradition. Some, satirized as "liberal reactionaries" and including Hu Shih and the Crescent Society, tried to maintain an equally difficult middle-of-the-road stand on tradition. Their attempts to compare the opposition between traditional and modern literature in China to the supposed dichotomy of European culture as either "classical" or "romantic" and to suggest that "there was something good in both" drew attacks on them as merely "keepers of peace and order."

Violent as were the attacks of Lu Hsün and Kuo Mo-jo against all suggestions for rehabilitating tradition, paradoxically both men could claim, in contrast to their younger contemporaries, a sound classical training. Lu Hsün wrote the first historical study of the Chinese novel. Kuo Mo-jo was an archeologist who had written books on ancient Chinese society and oracle bone inscriptions.

While Chinese tradition was thus vigorously attacked and feebly defended, importation from Western tradition was being carried out on a large scale. Translation was one of the important activities of the period, most of the periodicals dividing their pages evenly between translated and original works. It was only through imitating Western literature, it was maintained, that China could educate herself into producing a literature able to rival that of other nations. One should be wary, nevertheless, of oversimplification in speaking about Western influence. Most translations of other literatures, Russian and Scandinavian for example, popular as they were, were retranslations of English or Japanese translations. It would be difficult to find a piece of mature criticism of any Western literature: Most discussions rather were replete with misinterpretations or vague interpretations obtained through second-hand sources. The mere echoes of "naturalism" or of "romanticism" in an article by Mao Tun (1896-   ) or Kuo Mo-jo do not completely explain their literary positions.

During these ten years of productivity and controversy, Chinese writers flirted with practically every brand of Europeanism available since the nineteenth century, and finally espoused late nineteenth century realism (or naturalism—the terms were used interchangeably), qualified later as "socialist realism" or "neo-realism." Perhaps realistic works are more "translatable." The element of connotation is reduced to a minimum; even a weak translation will have some kind of cognitive value, giving at least sociological "information" and containing a "truth" reducible to conceptual terms. Discussion of Zola, Ibsen, or Turgenev, for example, centered on graspable "ideas" or social messages. They provided the most congenial models for a literary movement that had begun and that remained closely associated with social reform programs.

The general attitude was thus overwhelmingly in favor of Western imitation and against the inherited tradition, with all moderate compromises also categorically rejected. The tensions created by such extreme antitraditionalism are clearly discernible in the more specific theories and performances of the new literature of the 1920's. A closer investigation will be made of these three problems: (1) the concept of literature, its nature and its function; (2) the change in literary medium; and (3) the new status of the novel. Complex as the developments along these lines were, the basic transition from the Chinese tradition to the literary left is unmistakable.

Any concept of literature involves both its nature and function. The problem of what literature is and what it does was subject to intensive inquiry during the decade 1920-1930. It was of primary importance to defend the place and "use" of literature in a rapidly changing society. Traditionally, there had been obvious connections between literature, as one social institution, and other social institutions. Success in the civil service examination provided the man of letters with an official career and privileged social status. Through this regulating device, the aims of the artist-elite were identified with those of his society; his writings embodied its particular code of values. All literature existed, moreover, as part of a tradition initiated in the great Classics; it perpetuated its own particular conventions, rather than consciously attempting to "imitate nature" or "represent reality." Literature was a human activity distinct from other activities, and pattern, harmony, or decoration were its characteristic features. This concept was spacious enough to include what have come to be regarded in the West as marginal forms, forms written for nonaesthetic purposes, such as biographies, essays, letters, occasional verse, and official memorials. In other words, there was no theoretical tradition in China that narrowed the aesthetic function to specialized techniques in medium exploitation, or that emphasized the sheer disinterestedness of imaginative contemplation. Literature, to be serious at all, was a didactic instrument. This concept of the nature and function of literature was carried on into the modern literary movement, reappearing, however, in a completely new form.

Yet the Western emphasis on the purity of art was not without its representatives during the debate over the concept of literature in modern China. The Creation Society, led by the young Kuo Mo-jo, translator of the *Sorrows of Young Werther* and *Immensee,* dubbed themselves the "art for art's sake" group and clamored for originality and creativeness, claiming that the only standard in art was "its perfection and beauty." The members of the Literary Studies Society, on the other hand—the most influential group during the first half of the twenties, with Mao Tun as their most energetic spokesman—were united on a stand of "art for life's sake," and committed to a rather vague ideal of humanitarianism. Their favorite phrase was that literature should reflect the times. This insistence that literature had to be contemporaneous to be valid came to refer to a writer's awareness of specific social situations. Significantly enough, Kuo Mo-jo was then a practising poet, while Mao Tun was to become a novelist. Literature was even more definitely a tool of social reform for Lu Hsün, who turned from medicine to literature, convinced that the Chinese mind rather than the Chinese physique required medication—"Art should reform life."

Political events during the mid-twenties made it difficult for aloof "romanticism" and mild "humanitarianism" to maintain their stands. There was renewed resentment against Western imperialism, while Marxism was becoming a dominant factor in Chinese intellectual life. The purge of leftist writers beginning in 1927 was forcing final choices among indignant intellectuals. The Literary Studies Society was deserted by several writers for not taking a strong enough editorial position. The Creation Society went through a complete *volte-face* and began to raise the banner of revolutionary literature. Trotsky's *Literature and Revolution* was translated as a group project in 1926. Lu Hsün became leader of the Small Talk group, advocating a socialist realism yet attacking the reduction of all art to propaganda. A new group appeared, the Crescent Society, to argue a rationalistic position detached from incidental politics. Their leading poet was Hsü Chih-mo, translator of Katherine Mansfield, who had, according to Lu Hsün, wept at her grave. He was one of the leading experimenters with English metrical forms. Lu Hsün tried for a while to maintain a stand between this "ivory tower" group and the slogan thinkers of the transformed Creation Society. Towards 1929, he felt compelled by the literary controversies to study Soviet criticism, and retranslated the literary theories of Lunacharsky and Plekhanov from Japanese, supplying in fact a theoretical basis for the new proletarian literature movement. He became one of the leaders of the League of Leftist Writers, which also included Kuo Mo-jo and Mao Tun, upon its formation in 1930. The transition from the literary revolution to revolutionary literature was considered complete. The theory of "neo-realism" based on Marxist principles advocated by the League postulates a particularly correlative relationship between the nature and function of literature. The sporadic attempts of modern Chinese writers to define literature as an autonomous activity, after considerable floundering in Western terminology, were to be conclusively terminated. Art as a weapon in class struggle, was, in a sense, a return to the traditional Chinese concept of the didactic function of literature, while the artist, provided he identified his aims with those of his society, was again a being comfortably integrated within that society.

The most drastic departure from tradition was apparently the rehabilitation of the vernacular language. It is an extremely difficult and complex problem to assess the aesthetic significance of this shift in literary medium. How dependent is literary development on linguistic development? Linguistic studies have suggested that eighteenth-century English poetry, for example, was possible because the English language had become limpid and clear. An awareness of this dialectical relation between language and literature seems to be indicated in Hu Shih's slogan "a vernacular literature and a literary vernacular"; the emphasis on the necessity of literature to approximate the spoken language as directly as possible tended, however, to obscure the contrast that inevitably exists between the literary exploitation of linguistic resources and common everyday speech.

Both the script and grammar of the Chinese language were attacked by the reformers. Its cumbersome script was held accountable for China's ninety per cent illiteracy. Proposals to discard ideographs or "characters" in favor of a phonetic system nettled the pride of nationalists anxious to preserve the unique distinctions of a language which had evolved in such splendid isolation. No satisfactory solution has been reached and the problem is very much one for the future. Since the visual effect of the Chinese character was no longer, if indeed it ever had been, prominent in the total aesthetic meaning of any work, the reform of script was of less pertinence in literary discussions; the problem of syntactical style is clearly more germane to literary characteristics. Before competent studies of grammar had been made, the Chinese language was attacked for its ultra-analytical structure and the narrowness of its range. The "weight" of individual symbols, and the terseness and allusiveness of phrases, developed through the accumulation of a long tradition, moreover, made Chinese an intractable medium for expressing the precise nuances and relationships of foreign ideas. Even though the vernacular language approximated the structure of everyday speech and was less fettered by erudition, thus appearing to provide more freedom of expression, it was still regarded as inadequate. Some sort of Europeanization of syntax was deemed necessary.

The tremendous translating activities that were carried out in the decade after the Literary Revolution have inevitably had their effect on the Chinese language. All the major writers of this period devoted a great part of their energies to translation, and the effects are discernible in almost every one of their works. There is no question about the presence of the Westernized vocabulary. Failing to find Chinese equivalents for imported concepts, translators were compelled either to transliterate or to coin new compounds, thereby accelerating the polysyllabic tendency of the Chinese language. The Literary Studies Society held many discussions on the methods of translation, but a later attack on the awkwardness and unintelligibility of Lu Hsün's translations brought out what seems to be the heart of the matter. Lu Hsün defended himself on the grounds that not only new ideas but new ways of expression were necessary to the new literature. Importation and absorption of Western grammar and syntax, though clumsy in the beginning, would, in the long run, "force" into being a richer, more precise and more flexible Chinese language. In the short run, however, the use of this Westernized sentence structure resulted frequently in a language which, even while claiming to be written in the vernacular, actually did not approximate everyday speech and was intelligible only to a new elite acquainted with Western works. The "vulgarization of literature" movement inaugurated by the Leftist League in 1930, included a program to return to the living speech of the common people. Linguistic resources were to be augmented through the deliberate incorporation of dialectal expressions and local idioms. Thanks to the shifting nature of his medium, the modern Chinese writer, as compared with his predecessors of the last four or five centuries, has at his disposal a wider range of vocabulary and a more flexible grammatical style. He no longer relies solely on the memorization of classical texts to learn his literary language, nor is he committed to monotonous imitations of what has already been done in the past as well as it can be done. The literary potentialities of the new medium will not be realized, however, until writers can concretely demonstrate the imaginative heights of which it may be capable.

Since the Literary Revolution, there has appeared an imposing number of creative works in the vernacular. Poetic attempts have suffered most perhaps from starting in an unexploited medium with no preformed conventions. The drama has probably been the most vigorous of literary forms; as propaganda, its usefulness has been obvious. In spite of the completed naturalization of Western dramatic techniques, many attempts have been made to utilize historical or popular themes. The dramatic form, of necessity, makes more concessions to the habits and the taste of its wide audience. The novel, however, was the vehicle which engaged the literary efforts of most major writers. In their works, there has been little utilization of the accessible and highly developed native tradition of fiction.

This traditional novel, whose crude beginnings can be traced to at least the tenth century, was never before modern times acknowledged as serious literature; it had no critical status, being written in the colloquial language, and it was aurally intelligible. The novel had evolved from primitive oral traditions, but even after arrival at maturity it remained popular: It had to provide immediate pleasure to a wide audience in order to survive at all. When it came to be written, the artistic novel was modeled on these popular forms and preserved many of their structural characteristics. Relative lack of self-consciousness on the part of writers when using this form led to little technical experiment. The main bulk of fiction consisted of historical romances, picaresque tales, and family tragedies, with social problems or psychological studies treated only indirectly. Unlike the Western case, imaginative genres devoted solely to aesthetic purposes, were not regarded as the core of literary art. Chinese readers of the twentieth century were naturally surprised to discover the status accorded these forms in the West and were prompted to make enlightening investigations of these subtraditional genres. Because their subject matter lacked apparent relevance to reform, they were rejected as models for literary composition in favor of the realistic novel of the West. These early Chinese novels were considered, no doubt, to be at least as "useless" as Dante and Milton.

Both the "translatableness," the accessibility of the Western realistic novel, and its use as social document made it the model for widespread imitation. In the theme, setting, structure, and characterization of modern Chinese novels this particular influence is prevalent. Lu Hsün, considered the greatest figure in modern Chinese literature, is not primarily a writer of the novel or the short story; his position as the leader of the literary revolution is due to his translations and his numerous polemical writings. Through the latter he became involved in almost every literary controversy of his time. His theories are not easy to clarify, the main thread being woven into a maze of clever paradoxes and violent sarcasms. In his few creative works, he gives a penetrating depiction of Chinese peasant society, in a setting alive with local color, earthy details, and sardonic humor. His pitiless caricature, Ah Q, is an unforgettable denunciation of a despicable rustic vagabond, caught in the bewildering net of a changing society. Lu Hsün's short stories are often sketches of people, or "slices of life" with little complexity of plot, in the manner of Chekhov. Their substance usually resides in some sociological or psychological meaning. "My Home Town" (*Ku-hsiang*) contains a sympathetic portrait of the long-suffering Chinese peasant whose poignant situation is pointed up effectively by the contrast with the author's happier childhood memories. The unique texture of his writings is due to a brilliant exploitation of the possible nuances and twists of words.

Mao Tun, as the first editor of the organ of the Literary Studies Society, advocated a "humanitarian realism"; in his creative writings he accordingly acknowledged as his masters both Zola and Tolstoi. If he did not write the greatest novel of modern China, he deserves mention for having written, it seems to me, the most characteristic novel of the early phase of the literary movement. His work *Midnight; a romance of China in 1930* (*Tzu-yeh*) tries to demonstrate the thesis that capitalism is a dead-end road in China. The central figure is a would-be capitalist, the manager of a silk factory in Shanghai, self-confident and ruthless. The repercussions of world depression, the breakdown of rural society, labor agitation, civil war, and his own reckless speculations combine to bring about his downfall. Our interest is held not by the character and fortunes of its hero, but by the broad panorama in the novel which weaves in the threads from this complex historical background. There is strained melodrama and sordid detail, but the novel is memorable for certain carefully arranged scenes and for the balanced portrayal of the

realistic and the incongruous. His prose lacks the overtones and
resonances of Lu Hsün's style. There are no positive values in this
relentless book: The capitalists are unscrupulous and despicable;
the workers, a confused mob; the self-styled intellectuals, aloof,
ineffectual, and silly. It is easy to understand the criticism directed
against *Midnight* by the "revolutionary critics": The novel is too
depressing; it does not "point a way to the future."

After the ascendancy of "revolutionary literature" towards 1930,
the new novel became more "positive," more "constructive." The
earlier realism of Lu Hsün and Mao Tun was qualified by a proletarian world view. These new works claimed to be more realistic,
but the necessity of adhering to a specific evaluation of reality and
of conforming to one social doctrine tended to make the novel more
"idealistic" than "realistic." Compared with the popular novel of
the past, the new novel has gained in stature as a form of art; it has
tried to minimize its function as entertainment to become, as all
acknowledged classical literature had been, a form with serious
didactic and social purposes.

It would be premature to determine whether the new literary
products do indeed justify the Literary Revolution. Rejection of the
literary past entailed the transformation of the literary medium and
the introduction of new techniques. Tradition's inclusive concept
of literature and its integration of the artist into society, however,
in spite of Western inspiration and because of social pressure, have
reappeared in a new disguise. A conscious antitraditionalism was
undoubtedly the foremost motivation of the modern literary movement in China: The middle-of-the-road group studied Western
literature but was hesitant in its attitude toward the past, while the
extremists' stand on tradition, based on a genuine belief that the
Chinese literary tradition had reached a state of impasse, was decisive. Given the particular social circumstances, moreover, the leftist
outcome appears now to have been an inevitable development of
cultural iconoclasm.

Since 1949, antitraditional forces have been channeled officially
into the direction of "revolutionary literature." There have been
increasing signs, however, that the party line is advocating a return
to native Chinese tradition—what is referred to as the "people's
tradition." Writers formerly rejected as "dead," are being presented
as having been the spokesmen of the people's revolutionary aspirations. This reclaiming of at least a part of the Chinese past does not

necessarily indicate a pendulum reaction regarding the attitude toward tradition. It could rather imply a reconsideration of the transition, outlined in this paper, from the literary revolution to revolutionary literature. The new regime in China undoubtedly requires the recognition of a shared heritage to hold together a national structure. Yet the half-digested absorption of Western realism, for example, and the subsequent adoption of a proletarian literature may have been too hasty; it did not permit adequate experimentation or effective transmutation of Western literary techniques. The recent efforts to rehabilitate tradition may well represent a re-evaluation of the modern literary movement which so categorically rejected it.

SUGGESTED READINGS

MODERN CHINESE HISTORY

John K. Fairbank, *The United States and China*, rev. ed. (Cambridge, Mass.: Harvard University Press, 1958). (Also Compass Books #C108, 1962.)

O. Edmund Clubb, *Twentieth Century China* (New York: Columbia University Press, 1964).

Ssu-yü Teng and John K. Fairbank, *China's Response to the West* (Cambridge, Mass.: Harvard University Press, 1954). (Also Atheneum Paperbacks #44, 1963.)

Michael Greenberg, *British Trade and the Opening of China 1800-1842* (Cambridge: Cambridge University Press, 1951).

Arthur Waley, *The Opium War Through Chinese Eyes* (London: Allen & Unwin, 1958).

John K. Fairbank, *Trade and Diplomacy on the China Coast: the Opening of the Treaty Ports 1842-1854* (Cambridge, Mass.: Harvard University Press, 1953), 2 vols.

Mary C. Wright, *The Last Stand of Chinese Conservatism: The T'ung-chih Restoration, 1862-1874* (Stanford: Stanford University Press, 1957).

Lyon Sharman, *Sun Yat-sen* (New York: John Day, 1934).

SOCIETY AND ECONOMY

Hsiao-tung Fei, *Peasant Life in China: A Field Study of Country Life in the Yangtze Valley* (New York: Dutton, 1939).

R. H. Tawney, *Land and Labour in China* (London: Allen & Unwin, 1932).

Chung-li Chang, *The Chinese Gentry, Studies on Their Role in Nineteenth-Century Chinese Society* (Seattle: University of Washington Press, 1955).

Hsiao-tung Fei, *China's Gentry, Essays in Rural-Urban Relations* (Chicago: The University of Chicago Press, 1953).

Marion J. Levy, *The Family Revolution in Modern China* (Cambridge, Mass.: Harvard University Press, 1949).

Francis L. K. Hsu, *Under the Ancestors' Shadow: Chinese Culture and Personality* (New York: Columbia University Press, 1948).

C. D. Cowan, ed., *The Economic Development of China and Japan* (New York: Praeger, 1964).

G. C. Allen and Audrey Donnithorne, *Western Enterprise in Far Eastern Economic Development: China and Japan* (New York: Macmillan, 1954).

INTELLECTUAL AND CULTURAL LIFE

Joseph R. Levenson, *Confucian China and its Modern Fate: The Problem of Intellectual Continuity* (Berkeley: University of California Press, 1958). (Also Anchor Books #A391, 1964.)

Joseph R. Levenson, *Confucian China and its Modern Fate: The Problem of Monarchical Decay* (Berkeley: University of California Press, 1964).

Benjamin I. Schwartz, *In Search of Wealth and Power: Yen Fu and the West* (Cambridge: Harvard University Press, 1964).

Tse-tsung Chow, *The May Fourth Movement: Intellectual Revolution in Modern China* (Cambridge, Mass.: Harvard University Press, 1960) .

C. T. Hsia, *A History of Modern Chinese Fiction 1917-1957* (New Haven: Yale University Press, 1961).

Michael Sullivan, *Chinese Art in the Twentieth Century* (Berkeley: University of California Press, 1959).

CHINESE COMMUNISM AND COMMUNIST CHINA

Stuart R. Schram, *The Political Thought of Mao Tse-tung* (New York: Praeger, 1963).

Edgar Snow, *Red Star Over China* (New York: Random House, 1938).

Conrad Brandt, Benjamin Schwartz, and John K. Fairbank, *A Documentary History of Chinese Communism* (Cambridge, Mass.: Harvard University Press, 1952).

Benjamin I. Schwartz, *Chinese Communism and the Rise of Mao* (Cambridge, Mass.: Harvard University Press, 1951).

Robert C. North, *Moscow and the Chinese Communists* (Stanford: Stanford University Press, 1953; 2nd ed., 1963).

John Wilson Lewis, *Leadership in Communist China* (Ithaca: Cornell University Press, 1963) .

John Wilson Lewis, *Major Doctrines of Communist China* (New York: Norton, 1964).

A. Doak Barnett, *Communist China in Perspective* (New York: Praeger, 1962).

A. Doak Barnett, *Communist China and Asia, Challenge to American Policy* (New York: Harper, 1960). (Also Vintage Books #V185.)

Choh-ming Li, *Economic Development of Communist China: An Appraisal of the First Five Years of Industrialization* (Berkeley: University of California Press, 1959).

The China Quarterly (London, 1960-).